My Book

This book belongs to

Name: _____

©All rights reserved-Math-Knots LLC., VA-USA
www.math-knots.com

Grade 1
Vol 1
Index

Grade 1
Vol 1
Index

Copy right © 2019 MATH-KNOTS LLC

All rights reserved, no part of this publication may be reproduced, stored in any system or transmitted in any form, or by any means, electronic, mechanical, photocopying, recording, or otherwise without the written permission of MATH-KNOTS LLC.

Cover Design by :
Gowri Vemuri

First Edition :
August, 2023

Author :
Math-Knots LLC

Edited by :
Raksha Pothapragada

Questions: mathknots.help@gmail.com

NOTE : CCSSO or NCTM or VDOE is neither affiliated nor sponsors or endorses this product.

Dedication

This book is dedicated to:
My Mom, who is my best critic, guide and supporter.
To what I am today, and what I am going to become tomorrow,
is all because of your blessings, unconditional affection and support.

This book is dedicated to the
strongest women of my life ,
my dearest mom
and
to all those moms in this universe.

G.V.

Grade 1
Vol 1
Index

Week	Page No
Week 1	9-36
Week 2	37-70
Week 3	71-96
Week 4	96-122
Week 5	123-144
Week 6	145-166
Week 7	167-190
Week 8	191-212
Week 9	213-232
Week 10	233-252
Answer Keys	253-281

Grade 1
Volume 1
Week 1

Grade 1
Volume 1
Week 1

Level 1 - Week 1
Topics Covered Include:

Reading Comprehension
Writing
Vocabulary
Grammar

Grade 1
Volume 1
Week 1

SECTION 1 – Vocabulary

Write a sentence each using the words given below:

1. Paper :

   _____

   _____

   _____

   _____

2. Class :

   _____

   _____

   _____

   _____

3. Teacher :

   _____

   _____

   _____

   _____

Grade 1
Volume 1
Week 1

4. Group :

5. Add :

6. Land :

7. Glass :

8. Shall :

9. Wrap :

10. Catch :

11. Chapter :

Grade 1
Volume 1
Week 1

12. Bell :

_____

_____

_____

_____

13. Spell :

_____

_____

_____

14. Step :

_____

_____

_____

Grade 1
Volume 1
Week 1

15. Dress :

16. Chest :

17. Length :

18. Shelf :

_____

_____

_____

_____

SECTION 2 – Grammar

Statements, Questions and Commands

Statements: A sentence that says or states something is called a statement.

Example: I have lost my purse

Example: The baby is feeling cold.

Questions: A sentence that asks a question is called a question sentence.

Example: What is your name?

Example: How old are you?

Commands: A sentence that gives a command is called a command sentence.

Example: Open the window.

Example: Walk carefully.

1. Write **S** for statements, **Q** for questions and **C** for commands:

A. We really enjoyed the breakfast today. _____

B. Shall I get you a glass of water? _____

C. Please do not give me cold water. _____

D. Kindly show me some interesting novels. _____

E. I am fond of reading fiction. _____

F. What kind of books do you like? _____

G. Who brought these delicious strawberries? _____

H. Copy this exercise carefully. _____

I. Adam, go to the doctor. _____

J. Let's go play basketball. _____

K. The leaves are green in color. _____

L. Do I have to water the plants? _____

M. Go to the store. _____

N. Please shut the door after you enter. _____

O. Can you walk the dog? _____

Write three sentences – a statement, a question, and a command – about each of the following words:

2. Paper :

_____

_____

_____

3. Class :
_____
_____
_____

4. Teacher :
_____
_____
_____

5. Group :
_____
_____
_____

6. Add :
_____
_____
_____

7. Land :

8. Glass :

9. Shall :

10. Wrap :

11. Catch :

_____

_____

_____

12. Chapter :

_____

_____

_____

13. Bell :

_____

_____

_____

14. Spell :

_____

_____

_____

15. Step :

_____

_____

_____

_____

16. Dress :

_____

_____

_____

_____

17. Chest :

_____

_____

_____

_____

18. Length :

19. Shelf :

20. Fill :

21. Drink :

22. Thick:

23. Print:

24. Since:

25. Grip:

SECTION 3 - Reading Comprehension

Read the passage and answer the questions given below:

The largest bird in the world can't fly at all. They are so big that it has become impossible for them to fly. Instead of flying, they run. They have very powerful legs and can run almost as fast as a horse.

Ostriches live in the dry parts of Africa. They usually eat plants, but sometimes they eat small reptiles. They can even go for a long time without water if they have enough green plants to eat.

Ostriches live in groups of 5 to 50 birds. When scared, they will either hide themselves by lying flat against the ground, or run away. If cornered, it can attack with a kick of its powerful legs.

1. Answer the following:

   a. Why is it impossible for Ostriches to fly?

   _____

   _____

   _____

   _____

   _____

   _____

b. Write about the habitat of the Ostrich?

c. What do the Ostrich do when they are scared?

_____

_____

d. What do the Ostriches do when they are cornered?

_____

_____

_____

_____

2. **Write True or False for the following sentences:**

   a. Green plants help ostriches to live without water.

   _____

   b. Ostriches have very weak legs and so they cannot run fast.

   _____

   c. Ostriches live in dry parts of Africa.

   _____

3. **Write the definition of the following words:**

a. Powerful

_____

b. Attack

_____

c. Largest

_____

d. Impossible

_____

4. **Find a book in your library or your classroom about a rare bird and write facts about it:**

_____

_____

_____

_____

_____

_____

Read the passage and answer the questions given below:

The first garden strawberry was grown in Brittany in France during the late 18th century. A strawberry is a red, sweet, juicy fruit. Strawberries are usually eaten fresh. They have many medical uses as well.

They are used to make jams, pickles, ice creams, yogurts, smoothies and juices. The strawberry is the only fruit that has seeds on the outside. There are around 200 seeds in a strawberry. Strawberry flavors are also widely used in many products like lip gloss, candy, perfume, and many others.

In Sweden, strawberries are a traditional dessert. In Belgium, there is a strawberry museum. Strawberries are grown worldwide.

5. **Answer the following:**

   a. Have you ever eaten a strawberry? How is the taste?

   b. What are the uses of strawberry flavors?

c. Where do you find the seeds in a strawberry?

d. In which place was the first strawberry grown and where is the strawberry museum located?

6. Write two words to describe a strawberry.

   a. _____

   b. _____

7. Name two things that you can make using strawberries.

   a. _____

   b. _____

8. Give the definition of the following words:

   a. Values

   _____

   _____

   b. Traditional

   _____

   _____

   c. Museum

   _____

d. Medical value

_____

_____

9. **Write True or False for the following sentences:**

   a. Strawberries are bitter in taste.

   _____

   b. Strawberries are grown worldwide.

   _____

   c. Strawberries have medicinal values.

   _____

   d. Strawberries are blue in color.

   _____

   e. Strawberries are vegetables.

   _____

SECTION 4 – Writing

1. Write about your last school trip.

2. You have participated in your school sports day. Write about your participation in any of the sports event. Mention if you have received awards.

3. Going Green Challenge: Best out of Waste

Use recycled products (newspapers and magazines) to make amazing art projects.

Week 1- Puzzle 1 (Word Search)

Solve the following puzzle by finding all the hidden words!

```
G L A S S P E L L O L D E C L C H B C D L E
E P L T S E E D S L P P F T T E N G L S R O
S A E L E N G T H R A N L S E D N S S F O C
L P N E R L T T S D R H T L G G L E L A E G
H S L A D H H H P S H C S E F A C A C L A R
P S N N L A S P D A G S T L A P L W B G A S
E A A H P S R R E L T A E S H C T C S A C O
E L S G P T E L P U H H P H T H H O S T L D
A C S E E F P D C L S W P C A E U E S A S P
L S T C R R G L U P A L C O S E L A R S E H
H D A R L H T P E L L R E E L L P S R P H C
T G P F T A E L A D E L S U S R T S P P P P
E E E A L E L D D S G N L H S A E E R N T S
A H T S T R S W H P R L C W R S F D L T L S
N D R E U P R O C N O B R E L E A A C S R H
R T T P L L H D E N U A P C S E T C S G N A
A H S H L U A A G A P A U S W A N C D D S L
A D G H T W P S S H P G G H L L A H E A L S
E L T H S G D P E A C H D S E H S E C L O A
C P L S P D T D H S C F H T S A E S N T E P
A U F D A T T T R H A L P H T A E T L L A A
W C E B E L L H L L D C S H P R E T P A H C
```

Words List

DRESS	WRAP	CHAPTER
GLASS	ADD	CATCH
LAND	GROUP	CHEST
LENGTH	BELL	PAPER
SHELF	SPELL	CLASS
STEP	TEACHER	SHALL

Week 1 - Puzzle 2 (Word Scramble)

Unscramble the following list of shuffled words to meaningful words!

1. ESTP
2. DDA
3. BLEL
4. LHENTG
5. STEHC
6. RGOUP
7. TCCHA
8. SAGLS
9. SDSRE
10. PLLES
11. HPRECAT
12. EAHTCER
13. SLCSA
14. SLFHE
15. PRPEA
16. RWAP
17. NALD
18. HLASL

Level 1 - Week 2

Topics Covered Include:

Reading Comprehension
Writing
Vocabulary
Grammar

SECTION 1 – Vocabulary

Write 2 sentences each using the words given below:

1. Fill :

2. Drink :

3. Think :

4. Print :

5. Since :

6. Grip :

7. Wrist:

8. Doll:

9. Cross :

10. Block:

11. Strong :

12. Bottle :

13. Common :

14. Costume :

15. Body :

Grade 1
Volume 1
Week 2

16. Sheep :

_____

_____

_____

_____

17. Deer:

_____

_____

_____

_____

18. Source :

_____

_____

_____

_____

SECTION 2 – Grammar

Write three sentences – a statement, a question, and a command – about each of the following words:

1. Fill :

   _____

   _____

   _____

2. Drink :

   _____

   _____

   _____

3. Think :

   _____

   _____

4. Print :

5. Since :

6. Grip :

7. Wrist:

8. Doll:

9. Cross :

10. Block:

11. Strong :

12. Bottle :

13. Common :

14. Costume :

15. Body :

Grade 1
Volume 1
Week 2

_____

_____

_____

16. Sheep :

_____

_____

_____

17. Deer:

_____

_____

_____

18. Source :

_____

_____

_____

_____

19. Dictionary

_____

_____

_____

20. Giraffe

_____

_____

_____

21. Canteen

_____

_____

_____

_____

Negative Sentences: A sentence having **not** or **no** in it is called a negative sentence.

Example: We are **not** tired.
Example: He is **not** a liar.

Compare the following sentences:
   a. I am sad.
      I am **not** sad.

   b. He has some money.
      He has **no** money.

   c. She is skipping.
      She is **not** skipping.

   d. Close the windows.
      Don't/Do not close the windows.

22. Make the following sentences negative:

   a. His memory is sharp.

      _____

   b. My school is so far from my house.

      _____

   c. Water these plants daily.

      _____

d. Write fast.
_____

e. The dog is barking loudly.
_____

f. It is humid today.
_____

g. My mother is at home today.
_____

h. We can stand and talk here.
_____

i. The river was deep.
_____

j. She has a beautiful dress.
_____

k. Leave the room.
_____

l. I should see him.
_____

m. They have arrived.
_____

n. We have a holiday today.
_____

o. Sit down.
_____

p. He will leave today.
_____

q. I am happy.
_____

r. Peter can run fast.
_____

s. These questions are difficult.
_____

t. All these cars are for sale.
_____

SECTION 3 - Reading Comprehension

Read the passage and answer the questions given below:

The Telephone

In olden times, people used smoke signals, pigeons, horses and mail runners to send messages from one place to another.

These means of communication took a lot of time to deliver messages. If something happened to the pigeons, horses or mail runners, the messages would never reach their destination. Smoke signals were used to alert soldiers of danger but could create chaos if lit in the wrong way. Today, these old methods of communication are no longer used.

Now, there are easier methods to contact people, like the telephone or mobile phones. All we need to do is dial a number. These devices help us convey messages very quickly. The telephone is one of the most widely used devices in the world.

The telephone was invented by Alexander Graham Bell in the year 1876. He was a scientist and an inventor. He was very curious about how electricity worked. In the 19th century, the telegraph was popular. Messages were sent through a single wire using the telegraph.

Later, Bell invented a device that could transmit words. It was named the telephone. It was the first device that allowed people to talk to each other while being in two different places.

Did you know that the first telephone did not have a bell? The caller had to tap the phone with a hammer. The receiver, at the other end, would know that there was an incoming call.

The telephone was not Bell's only invention. He also invented the photo phone. On April 3, 1973, the mobile phone was invented by Martin Cooper. Today, mobile phones are one of our favorite communication devices. We use them to talk to our friends, send text messages, play games, listen to music and watch videos.

1. **Answer the following:**

   a. What did people use in the olden times to communicate?

   _____

   _____

   _____

   _____

   _____

   _____

   b. What were the differences between old and new means of communication?

   _____

   _____

   _____

c. What are Graham Bell's other inventions?

d. Why are the older methods no longer used?

e. How did the users of the first telephone know they were receiving a call?

f. What are the differences between the first telephone and mobile phones?

2. Write True or False for the following sentences:

a. The telephone was Graham Bell's only invention.

_____

b. Mobile phones are used only to talk to our friends.

_____

c. Graham Bell invented the telegraph.

_____

d. The first telephone had a bell.

_____

3. Write the definition of the following words:

a. Communication

_____

_____

b. Destination

_____

_____

c. Chaos

_____

d. Scientist

e. Inventor

f. Device

g. Transmit

4. Go to your library and read about any inventor and his/her invention. Write a few facts about it.

Grade 1
Volume 1
Week 2

_____

_____

_____

_____

_____

5. If you want to invent a new means of communication, what would you invent?

_____

_____

_____

_____

_____

_____

_____

_____

6. Use a dictionary to find the difference between an inventor and discoverer. Write about any discoverer and his/her discovery.

Grade 1
Volume 1
Week 2

_____

_____

_____

SECTION 4 – Writing

1. Describe your neighborhood. Write about your friends and the games you play.

2. Write about your recent favorite dream.

3. Go Green Challenge: Turn it off.

Let us try to conserve electricity by turning off the lights and air conditioners when not in use in our homes and classrooms.

Why should we conserve electricity? It is important to conserve electricity because the **natural resources** that provide sources for electricity are being **depleted** quickly. Conserving electricity also **saves** money.

Week 2 - Puzzle 1 (Word Search)

Solve the following puzzle by finding all the hidden words!

```
T I K T S B O C H D I W M E R D I C G R P H
E B N D N T F S K C L S K R R I E C E I T T
T T R K N T E L P F C O E N P L S U O T L G
I T P I T R S T L G D U E T T R L I S S P S
E M U T S O C Y S I I R R O S L D D P E C C
I N O C T S K E D I F C O H E G T T S M M S
T D H W R S M E U O R E I C R E L B R L O I
T I U M O D C O S Y B W O I C T L C F K U E
L O I C N O S S I T I E P L C K M D B R S S
L O I O G O O I R I N L I P L B O Y E C R K
G R R G O O M B P I O O E D O O T E D B O O
O O O D C T C M E K S C O T S L D S N T P N
R O R S G U E O O D S D T O U I S H E E P S
E T P S E H U D P C N L P T C D N C T K I G
R C E I N E M M R C E G R F C O M C L R C C
R P B C O I S F S I E B L R C R I I E D D Y
C D O L W L P S I C N U H E K D R T G T B R
N G I P O G O E S P O K B T C I C N H R B G
N S R D T R R S R L I G P O O R C I L L L R
N U I F C B S E N D O R S R L C C R D R T O
U H P G O P I P R W C I L K B K E P C F I F
E W R K T O G K L I L C L U S S I S N E G U
```

Words List

WRIST	DRINK	CROSS
FILL	BOTTLE	STRONG
THICK	DEER	GRIP
BODY	SHEEP	BLOCK
COSTUME	SOURCE	PRINT
SINCE	COMMON	DOLL

Week 2 - Puzzle 1 (Word Search)

Solve the following puzzle by finding all the hidden words!

```
T I K T S B O C H D I W M E R D I C G R P H
E B N D N T F S K C L S K R R I E C E I T T
T T R K N T E L P F C O E N P L S U O T L G
I T P I T R S T L G D U E T T R L I S S P S
E M U T S O C Y S I I R R O S L D D P E C C
I N O C T S K E D I F C O H E G T T S M M S
T D H W R S M E U O R E I C R E L B R L O I
T I U M O D C O S Y B W O I C T L C F K U E
L O I C N O S S I T I E P L C K M D B R S S
L O I O G O O I R I N L I P L B O Y E C R K
G R R G O O M B P I O O E D O O T E D B O O
O O O D C T C M E K S C O T S L D S N T P N
R O R S G U E O O D S D T O U I S H E E P S
E T P S E H U D P C N L P T C D N C T K I G
R C E I N E M M R C E G R F C O M C L R C C
R P B C O I S F S I E B L R C R I I E D D Y
C D O L W L P S I C N U H E K D R T G T B R
N G I P O G O E S P O K B T C I C N H R B G
N S R D T R R S R L I G P O O R C I L L L R
N U I F C B S E N D O R S R L C C R D R T O
U H P G O P I P R W C I L K B K E P C F I F
E W R K T O G K L I L C L U S S I S N E G U
```

Words List

WRIST	DRINK	CROSS
FILL	BOTTLE	STRONG
THICK	DEER	GRIP
BODY	SHEEP	BLOCK
COSTUME	SOURCE	PRINT
SINCE	COMMON	DOLL

Grade 1
Volume 1
Week 3

Teacher English Booklet

Level 1 - Week 3

Topics Covered Include:

Reading Comprehension
Writing
Vocabulary
Grammar

SECTION 1 – Vocabulary

Write a sentence each using the words given below:

1. Luck :

2. Drum:

3. Bunch :

Grade 1
Volume 1
Week 3

4. Hundred :

5. Crush :

6. Summer :

Grade 1
Volume 1
Week 3

7. Suppose :

8. Late :

9. Bite :

10. Dime :

_____

_____

_____

_____

11. Smile :

_____

_____

_____

_____

12. Life:

_____

_____

_____

_____

13. Shape :

14. Bathe :

15. Phone :

16. History :

17. Ruby :

18. Freeze :

SECTION 2 – Grammar

1. Make the following sentences negative:

   a. I have some money in my purse.

   _____

   b. Sit in the open.

   _____

   c. He is speaking the truth.

   _____

   d. I had kept those chocolates for you.

   _____

e. I will go to the market tomorrow.

_____

_____

f. Give me milk and bread.

_____

_____

g. Close the windows.

_____

_____

h. She is writing neatly.

_____

_____

Interrogative Sentences: A sentence that asks a question is called an interrogative sentence.

Compare the following sentences:

a. I am right.
   Am I right?

b. She can help me.
   Can she help me?

c. You have a smile.
   Do you have a smile?

Grade 1
Volume 1
Week 3

2. Make the following sentences interrogative:

   a. We are late.
   _____

   b. She is old.
   _____

   c. The sound was clear.
   _____

   d. His clothes were dirty.
   _____

   e. She had a watch.
   _____

   f. They have seen the White House.
   _____

   g. He will leave early.
   _____

   h. The meeting is at 6pm.
   _____

i. The road to the station is narrow and bumpy.

_____

j. She has two sisters.

_____

k. She will be rewarded for her honesty.

_____

l. You should believe him.

_____

m. The boys are reading books.

_____

n. That snake was dangerous.

_____

o. My sister is very fond of music.

_____

p. He can drive a car.

_____

q. The telephone bell is ringing.

_____

r. These diamonds are real.

_____

s. The workers were faithful to the company.

_____

t. Somebody is knocking at the door.

_____

SECTION 3 - Reading Comprehension

Read the passage and answer the questions given below:

Helen Keller was only two years old when she became blind and deaf. Her world turned dark, silent, lonely, and very sad.

Ms. Sullivan began teaching Helen. At that time Helen was only five, her teacher taught her to read and write in Braille. Braille has patterns of raised dots that can be felt with fingertips. Teacher and pupil worked very hard. Neither teaching nor learning was easy. But when Helen was sixteen she could speak five languages!

Later, she went to college, wrote books, and did a lot of work to help the blind and the deaf.

Beethoven is the greatest musician of all times. He began to lose his hearing at an early age and became totally deaf at the age of 44. But the loss of hearing did not stop him from composing and playing music for people to enjoy.

Stephen Hawking is the greatest physicist in the world. He has a rare disability that has paralyzed him over these years. But he did not give up and he achieved great success in the field of physics. He has won many awards including the Presidential Medal of Freedom.

1. Answer the following:

   a. How was Helen Keller different from others?

b. How did Ms. Sullivan teach Helen? Describe it?

c. Why is Beethoven's music special?

d. What did Stephen Hawking do that inspires us?

2. Have you seen such people with special abilities? Write about them here.

3. Write the definitions for the following words:

   a. Pattern

   b. Compose

   c. Disability

   d. Paralyzed

Read the passage and answer the questions given below:

Save the Earth

The earth has been very kind to us. It has gifted us with nature. We go on taking from nature to make our lives comfortable. Do we ever give something in return? Do we realize that nature needs to be looked after? Nature has a system. By taking way too much of something from nature, we disturb its balance.

By polluting the air and water we harm nature and the earth. Pollution is harming animals, plants, water, mountains, deserts and even man. Plants help in cleaning the polluted air. For each tree we cut, three more should be planted. Plants also help to lessen noises around us. We are slowly killing the earth by deforesting or cutting down trees for building houses. We need to plant more trees to save the earth.

4. Answer the following:

a. How is pollution harmful?

_____
_____
_____
_____
_____
_____

b. How do plants help in reducing pollution?

_____
_____
_____
_____
_____
_____

c. What are the other ways to save the earth?

_____
_____
_____
_____
_____
_____

5. **Fill in the blanks with the words given below.**
   Ecosystem, dirty, spaces, mother, fertile.

   a. If we _____ our rivers, we will have no water to drink.

   b. The Earth cares for us as a _____ cares for her children.

   c. Earthworms make our gardens _____

   d. By taking away too much of something from nature, we disturb Earth's _____

   e. Our cities need many greener _____

6. Cutting of trees and hunting of animals have made many animals disappear. The lives of many more are in danger. Solve the jumbled words to find out some of the names:

   a. Eritg : _____

   b. Orcesnhrio : _____

c. Antgi apnad : _____

d. Dkuc : _____

e. Flwo : _____

f. Tnephela : _____

g. Npneiug : _____

7. Think and write:

Things I will do to improve my environment:
a. Grow more plants

b. _____

c. _____

d. _____

e. _____

f. _____

SECTION 4 – Writing

1. What makes your parents so special?

2. Write about your favorite book?
3. Earthworms make our gardens fertile. Don't kill them.

   Instead make earthworm manure with kitchen waste.

   Collect vegetable and fruit peels. Keep them in a container.

   Add the bio-waste (peels of vegetables and fruits) to your garden soil.

   A few days later you will see earthworms and they

   will make your garden fertile.

Week 3 - Puzzle 1 (Word Search)

Solve the following puzzle by finding all the hidden words!

```
L R H L S E U U H I T P E U S E C F E B E A
A I E D Z R U B Y F L I L M N B T S E F I L
E B S F N I U E T A E R S Y L U M E B C U U
Y I F E R H S E E U M E Y R O T S I H R I T
M R O R L E E S U P P O S E P A H S E I E Y
P B L E K S E I P S H E H U S H P E S C B D
E E T A L R I Z S S U S K F D M A M E T P N
S H R E M B L Y E U I H I R M H E U E M E H
M U L U E T R S N U D H C P R D R U M O N R
E L E N E O M T O D Z E L N I D P P R A E R
E C P O S I B E H T A B E Y U S Y U C U L P
R C U E L N O Y P H S T C E S B D T E L S O
K E S E S S C L E O I B M D H C C N B N T U
P I M I O I A P E B I E T U A P E Y D E D T
S M R M L S N D P E E D E M H E A E H L C H
P H P U U S R K H D S T E E L H R T L E Y I
I T U E H S R I D I S D F C C D C S R H D H
I M M I C S T R N R M E E R N T P E U B S P
H I N M H N D Y N R D C R U B S E S E Y R D
D A L I A D S F L U C K H S B P D O B E P D
E U L E H E K B R C S E M H E E L Y I I M R
N P P E S E P U D H U I D I L D E T S M P D
```

Words List

BATHE	HUNDRED	BITE
DRUM	LIFE	BUNCH
SHAPE	PHONE	LUCK
FREEZE	CRUSH	DIME
HISTORY	SMILE	SUMMER
RUBY	SUPPOSE	LATE

Week 3 - Puzzle 2 (Word Scramble)

Unscramble the following list of shuffled words to meaningful words!

1. FIEL
2. IDEM
3. EIBT
4. LMSEI
5. HBNCU
6. REMMSU
7. CSUHR
8. TEAL
9. BYRU
10. UMDR
11. SPHAE
12. UDREHND
13. BTEHA
14. ZFEEER
15. RYTSOHI
16. PUSEPOS
17. LKCU
18. HNOPE

Grade 1
Volume 1
Week 4

Teacher English Booklet

Level 1 - Week 4

Topics Covered Include:

Reading Comprehension
Writing
Vocabulary
Grammar

SECTION 1 – Vocabulary

Write a sentence each using the words given below:

1. Hair:

2. Stairs :

3. Wheel :

Grade 1
Volume 1
Week 4

4. Dream :

5. Peace :

6. Piece :

7. Throat :

8. Hard :

9. Morning :

10. Score :

11. Person :

12. Third :

13. During :

14. Burn :

15. Juice :

16. Guy:

_____

_____

_____

_____

17. Wishes:

_____

_____

_____

_____

18. Deer :

_____

_____

_____

_____

SECTION 2 – Grammar

1. Convert these sentences to interrogative sentences.

a. Sara will come tomorrow.
_____

b. Anthony won the competition.
_____

c. The bulls had managed to escape.
_____

d. They have climbed the mountain together.
_____

e. Brad is crossing the street.
_____

2. Write 4 kinds of sentences (Statements, Commands, Negative and Interrogative) using the words given below:
Example: Honest
Statement: Mark is an honest person
Command: Please be honest.
Negative: Sally is not honest.
Interrogative: Is he an honest person?

a. Beautiful

Statement:_____

Command: _____

Negative: _____

Interrogative: _____

b. Wisdom

Statement: _____

Command: _____

Negative: _____

Interrogative: _____

c. Gift

Statement: _____

Command: _____

Negative: _____

Interrogative: _____

d. Book

Statement: _____

Command: _____

Negative: _____

Interrogative: _____

Vowels and Consonants
There are 26 letters in English alphabet. Out of them there are five vowels and twenty one consonants.

Vowels: a, e, i, o, u
Consonants: b, c, d, f, g, h, j, k, l, m, n, p, q, r, s, t, v, w, x, y, z

3. **Mark the vowels only (circle or underline):**

   b, c, e, f

   s, w, t, a

   o, r, y, x

   m, n, p, i

   f, u, v, z

   q, v, g, e

   y, l, o, w

Grade 1
Volume 1
Week 4

4. Mark the consonants only(circle or underline):

   a, e, i, d

   c, i, o, u

   a, e, j, o

   x, o, u, a

   u, v, a, e

   e, i, a, p

   u, i, g, e

5. Fill in the blanks with correct vowels and learn the spellings:

   a. P _____ RR _____ T

   b. Q _____ N

   c. B _____ TT _____ R

   d. L _____ PT _____ P

   e. H _____ RS _____

   f. C _____ MP _____ SS

   g. T _____ L _____ PH _____ N _____

   h. C _____ B

Grade 1
Volume 1
Week 4

6. **Complete the words with correct vowels using the hints and learn the spellings:**

   a. _____ PPL _____ (a fruit)

   b. _____ MBR _____ LL _____ (we use it during rain)

   c. F _____ NG _____ R (part of our body)

   d. P _____ G _____ N (a bird)

   e. SCH _____ L (we go here to study)

   f. SH _____ S (We wear them on our feet)

7. **Complete the words with correct consonants using the hints and learn the spellings:**

   a. O _____ IO _____ (a vegetable)

   b. _____ I _____ EA _____ E (a juicy fruit)

   c. _____ EA _____ O _____ (a colorful bird)

   d. _____ A _____ E (birthdays are incomplete without eating this)

   e. _____ UI _____ A _____ (a musical instrument)

   f. _____ OO _____ (we use it to eat our meals)

SECTION 3 - Reading Comprehension

Read the passage and answer the questions given below:

Recycling Plastic

The world uses tons of plastic every day. It is used for various purposes like making toys, packaging products and so on. Massive amounts of it end up in the oceans. Plastic pollution has put the world's ocean and marine life at great risk. It is harming our ecosystem too. If we take action now, we can still save our marine ecosystem.

Recycling is a process where waste materials are used to produce a fresh supply of the same material. All waste materials cannot be recycled. When we dispose waste it is important to separate recyclable waste from non-recyclable waste. Recyclable waste can be put to good use without harming the environment. Plastic is a recyclable waste. Let us find out how plastic is recycled.

1. Collecting: Plastic bottles are collected along with other plastic waste from schools, houses, hospitals, restaurants and other places. They are then taken to a recycling center.

2. Sorting: First, the bottles and other containers are cleaned. Then, they are sorted according to the type of plastic and color. Each set is then sent to a shredding machine.

3. Melting: The plastic are washed to remove impurities. Then, they are dried and melted.

4. Flaking: The plastic is then shaped into thin flakes. The flakes are again washed and dried.

5. End product: The flakes can now be turned into many fine strings, which can be used to make a wide variety of products like clothes, carpets and so on. They can also be made into plastic bottles.

6. Answer the following:

1. Write a few ways in which you can reuse plastics?

_____

_____

_____

_____

_____

_____

_____

2. Write about other products that can be recycled apart from plastics.

_____

_____

3. What will happen if you don't recycle plastic?

4. Why is it important to separate recyclable waste from non-recyclable waste?

_____

_____

_____

_____

_____

5. Fill in the blanks:

a. Plastic bottles are collected along with other plastic waste from _____, houses, hospitals, _____, and other places.

b. They are then taken to a _____.

c. The bottles and other containers are _____. Then, they are sorted according to the type of _____ and _____

d. Each set is then sent to a _____ machine.

e. The _____ are used to make various products.

6. Write definitions of the following words:

a. Massive

_____

b. Pollution

_____

c. Ecosystem

_____

d. Dispose

_____

e. Sorted

_____

f. Impurities

_____

g. Shred

_____

Read the passage and answer the questions given below:

Rain in Summer
How beautiful is the rain!
After the dust and the heat,
In the broad and fiery street,
In the narrow lane.
How beautiful is the rain!

How it clatters along the roofs,
Like the tramps of hoofs!
How it gushes and struggles out,
From the throat of the overflowing spout!

Across the window pane
It pours and pours;
And swift and wide,
With a muddy tide,
Like a river down the gutter roars,
The rain, the welcome rain!

- Henry Wadsworth Longfellow

7. Answer the following:

a. How does the poet describe summer?

_____

_____

_____

_____

b. What do you do when you cannot go out due to heavy rains?

_____

_____

_____

_____

c. What changes do you notice in your surroundings soon after it stops raining?

_____

_____

_____

_____

8. Write definitions of the words given below and use those words to form sentences.
   a. Fiery

_____

_____

b. Clatter

_____

_____

c. Swift

_____

_____

d. Gush

_____

_____

e. Tramps

_____

_____

f. Hoofs

_____

_____

SECTION 4 – Writing

1. If you could live anywhere on earth, where would it be?

2. Write about your favorite movie or cartoon character.

3. Going Green Challenge: Reuse and Recycle

   Make a list of all the products you can reuse (Example: Water Bottles) and try to reuse them.

   Make a list of all the disposable items in your house that can be recycled and divide them into recyclable and non-recyclable waste.

Week 4 - Puzzle 1 (Word Search)

Solve the following puzzle by finding all the hidden words!

```
P B S Y N R E L C G L P O P I R U H S E Y R
I U U C P R S E D C A R O R R I G R E T D S
H R R I I M H E I D S D E H U S N O N G T H
I N O C O T P E Y D G G O R U I I I A I H I
E P N M I A R R R T D I D E C U N D R S N M
S R H P A C P A S P S D P U G S R A S T N D
G H A I I I R R S W A S Y H I E O H W B R R
I A N E H C R D I H Y E P I M C M S R R U E
I R D B S E E W R D U N U N D I H N S C I D
U D N N C O R H E N N I T D R P I R H H Y A
A T S I I N E E G E L O I T I H I A U B E W
H M U A N E R E E I H C S E H A I E T H M R
H J D I D G O L S E P E N R T R H R R H U E
I E R A H R C P A D A A J S E I O I D O R M
O I W A E R S U I A A S A H E P L A D R E S
E S U M E E A C D E E U R I E P P A T E E E
I S E H S I W I G D C S O C O E C B R R P N
R E S T E H H U U D R E A M R N A P D A T A
W T T A I E Y T O A C E D I I R E U H U T R
A R R R E C R C R E P D H O B S H I G U T I
I H E E H B R P W I H N P E P E E S S S O A
P N I U H H G I G D E B D U R I N G C R R I
```

Words List

WHEEL	PERSON	GUY
DEER	THROAT	PIECE
DREAM	PEACE	SCORE
BURN	THIRD	HARD
WISHES	MORNING	HAIR
STAIRS	JUICE	DURING

Week 4 - Puzzle 2 (Word Scramble)

Unscramble the following list of shuffled words to meaningful words!

1. EONSPR
2. EHWSIS
3. TDRHI
4. IRSTAS
5. IMRNOGN
6. IDNGRU
7. YUG
8. RBUN
9. JUIEC
10. DERE
11. RADH
12. AOHTTR
13. HRIA
14. CPEAE
15. PEICE
16. ERSOC
17. EEWLH
18. READM

Grade 1 Volume 1 Week 5

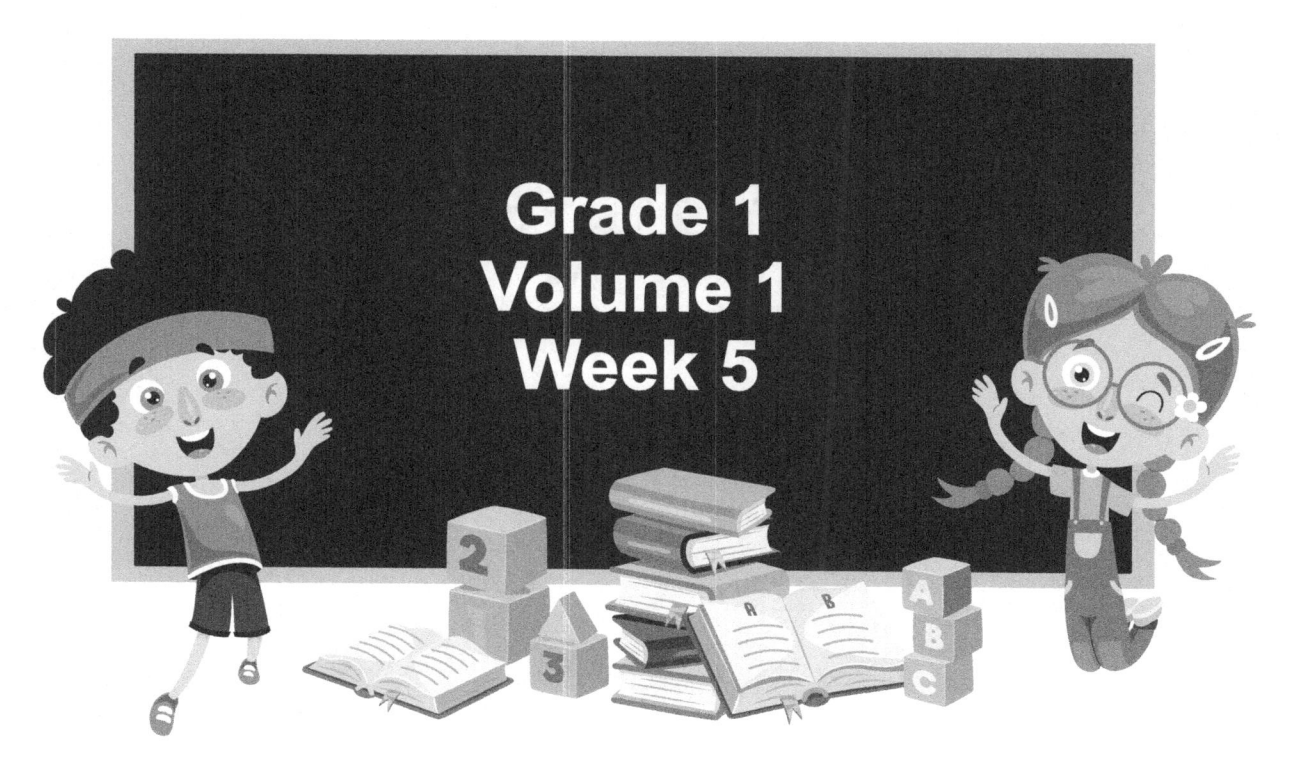

Teacher English Booklet

Level 1 - Week 5

Topics Covered Include:

Reading Comprehension
Writing
Vocabulary
Grammar

SECTION 1 – Vocabulary

Guess the word for the given definitions. Also form two sentences each using the word.

1. An instrument that transfers sound from one person to another. It is the basic means of communication.

   _____

   _____

2. The male species of horned animals like the deer, reindeer, and antelopes.

   _____

   _____

3. A small insect.

   _____

   _____

4. To take or keep a firm hold of something.

   _____

   _____

5. A dessert usually served on birthdays and festivals. It has different flavors.

   _____

   _____

Write 2 sentences each using the words given below:

6. Room :

   _____

   _____

   _____

   _____

7. Foot :

   _____

   _____

   _____

   _____

8. Loud :

   _____

   _____

   _____

   _____

9. Thousand:

10. Noise :

11. Boil :

12. Enjoy:

13. Ice :

14. Center :

15. Office :

16. Certain :

17. Giant :

18. Age :

19. Bridge :

20. Lunch :

21. Mix :

22. Berries

23. Sleeve:

_____

_____

SECTION 2 – Grammar

1. **Mark the vowels only (Circle or underline) :**

   u, f, j, d

   n, p, e, f

   h, l, m, o

   c, i, r, h

   a, v, n, s

   p, r, i, m

   s, a, j, n

2. **Fill in the blanks with appropriate vowels and learn the spellings:**

   a. C _____ P   (we use this to drink tea or coffee)

   b. _____ GL _____ _____   (home of Eskimos)

   c. _____ CT _____ P _____ S   (a water animal with many tentacles)

   d. D _____ _____ SY   (a flower)

Grade 1
Volume 1
Week 5

e. SH _____ _____ P   (this animal gives us wool)

f. F _____ R _____   (this element causes burns)

g. B _____ TT _____ RY   (a portable energy supplier)

3. **Fill in the blanks with appropriate vowels and learn the spellings:**

a. _____ I _____ _____ O _____ A _____ E

   (used to warm food)

b. I _____ E _____ _____ EA _____   (a dessert that is served cold)

c. _____ _____ AI _____ _____ A _____ E

   (used to move from one floor to another)

d. _____ U _____ E _____ _____ E _____ OE _____

   (Superman, Batman and the Avengers are called this)

e. E _____ E _____ _____ A _____ _____

   (A large grey animal with a trunk)

f. _____ E _____   (Used to open locked doors)

g. _____ A _____ I _____ _____ (

   The people closest to you. You live with them)

SECTION 3 - Reading Comprehension

Read the passage and answer the questions given below:

Malala Yousafzai

Malala Yousafzai was born on July 12, 1997. She is a Pakistani activist for female education and the youngest Noble Prize winner. She is known for her fight for human rights towards education for women in Pakistan, at the time when girls were banned from attending school.

In 2009, Malala wrote a blog detailing her life during the Taliban occupation. The following summer, New York Times made a documentary about her life as the Pakistani military intervened in the region. Malala had given interviews in print and on television post the documentary.

In October 2012, Yousafzai was injured after a Taliban gunman attempted to kill her. The incident sparked a national and international outpouring of support for Malala. After recovering, Yousafzai became an education activist. Yousafzai founded the Malala Fund, a non-profit organization and in 2013 she co-authored a book titled "I am Malala".

In 2014, Malala was awarded a Nobel Peace Prize for her struggle against the suppression of children and young people and for the rights of all children to education.

On July 12 2013, Malala's 16th birthday, she spoke at the United Nations to call for worldwide access to education. The event was later known as "Malala Day". It was her first public speech since the attack. Malala also presented "The Education We Want", a youth resolution of education demands written by Youth for Youth.

On July 12 2015, her 18th birthday, Malala opened a school in Lebanon, near the Syrian border, for Syrian refugees. The school is funded by the not-for-profit Malala Fund and offers education and training to girls aged 14 to 18 years. Malala called on world leaders to invest in "books, not bullets".

1. Answer the following:

   a. Who is Malala Yousafzai and what are her achievements?

   _____
   _____
   _____
   _____
   _____
   _____
   _____
   _____

   b. Why was she awarded the Nobel Peace Prize?

   _____
   _____
   _____
   _____
   _____
   _____

c. What are your views on education?

d. Do you think we need more people like Malala Yousafzai, and why?

Grade 1
Volume 1
Week 5

_____
_____
_____
_____

2. **Write the definitions for the following words:**

   a. Activist

   _____

   b. Blog

   _____

   c. Occupation

   _____

   d. Documentary

   _____

   e. Intervened

   _____

   f. Suppression

   _____

g. Resolution

_____

h. Refugees

_____

i. Banned

_____

j. Attempted

_____

3. If you were to get a Nobel Peace Prize, what would it be for?

_____

_____

_____

Read the poem given below and answer the following questions:

The Pedlar's Caravan

I wish I lived in a caravan
With a horse to drive, like a pedlar-man!
Where he comes from nobody knows,
Or where he goes to, but on he goes.

His caravan has windows two,
And a chimney of tin that the smoke comes through;
He has a wife, and a baby brown,
And they go riding from town to town.

Chairs to mend, and delft to sell!
He clashes the basins like a bell;
Tea-trays, baskets ranged in order,
Plates, with the alphabet round the border.

- W. B. Rands

4. Write True or False for the following sentences:

   a. The pedlar was married. _____

   b. He had to cook outside. _____

   c. He had no children. _____

   d. He could make a fire inside the caravan. _____

   e. He could see out of the caravan. _____

Select the correct answer from the given options:

5. Where had the caravan come from?
    a. No one can tell.
    b. From the Land of the Nod.
    c. From over the sea.

6. How did it move from place to place?
    a. It was a motor caravan.
    b. It was drawn by a horse.
    c. It was a trailer behind a car.

7. What kind of person lived in the caravan?
    a. A rich merchant.
    b. A man on holiday.
    c. A man selling things.

8. What were the plates like?
    a. Plain white.
    b. Blue all over.
    c. Decorated with letters.

9. How can we say that the pedlar was able to mend things?

_____

_____

10. Write the definitions of the following words:

    a. Caravan

    _____

    b. Pedlar

    _____

c. Chimney

_____

d. Delft

_____

SECTION 4 – Writing

1. Describe the picture given below and write about it:

Image obtained from search results for American Museum of Natural History^

2. Imagine and describe the Disney world in your own words.

3. Going Green Challenge: Separate the waste

Let us separate the waste produced in our houses into **organic waste, in-organic waste and recyclable products.**

Organic waste: Vegetable peels, fruits, flowers, etc.

In-organic waste: Chemicals, bones, etc

Recyclable: Bottles, Papers, etc

Why? To provide **proper disposal** of the vast amount of garbage produced in an **eco-friendly** manner. Different types of waste have different properties, and grouping them by type allows for proper processing or storage of the waste.

Week 5 - Puzzle 1 (Word Search)

Solve the following puzzle by finding all the hidden words!

```
R V N N R R C E T L C O E E L O L E I S S O
S N O I E I D D I E O D I O C E X E I E E E
C N M T I Y E N O D R T U O C C E T I L M H
H C N U L E O E A R I D A I N B E T B S O T
O E F O S D E J N S O E R S D C O R L I O B
C E S O N O E F N T U I S T A I N D D V R C
D O R N X E E T R E F O O G N D N I J L E E
T N R A R I O O C U I H H U E L B M N M R A
N E L N I E A O I S E T R T A E M N S O O G
L E O N F E Y V N E I N O U R M F G I A N T
I N C L O E E F U B E R R I E S O U R I I E
F L B E C C O T E V E E L S N D E N G A O B
N I H R O T R I O R C I H T N O E E I E T E
C N L F M O R F L O I D O N C T J G O L R I
C E G R R J T O L I F B S R A O A U C A R C
R T O B G U E E T N F I E H R N E R E A T E
I B A I N E F M B N O C E D O J C N C R G U
E L U B V A L I I T I S O O L C L I I R L E
O U A G X L N T N X N R G G E O U G O I N E
N E T O C R O S H U A I B R I D G E S I O N
T E F I A E O U A G S C E C N B U A E O X M
T S A I A T N I A T R E C V C C B M L H F E
```

Words List

CERTAIN	ROOM	AGE
BOIL	NOISE	OFFICE
THOUSAND	GIANT	ENJOY
ICE	MIX	CENTER
BERRIES	SLEEVE	LOUD
BRIDGE	FOOT	LUNCH

Week 5 - Puzzle 2 (Word Scramble)

Unscramble the following list of shuffled words to meaningful words!

1. OMOR
2. NEJYO
3. CEI
4. EAG
5. IACTNRE
6. NHCLU
7. OBIL
8. IRBERSE
9. NAGTI
10. OTOF
11. HDOAUSTN
12. LEEEVS
13. OUDL
14. XIM
15. IFFEOC
16. SOEIN
17. DGEIRB
18. NTECRE

Grade 1
Volume 1
Week 6

Teacher English Booklet

Level 1 - Week 6

Topics Covered Include:

**Reading Comprehension
Writing
Vocabulary
Grammar**

SECTION 1 – Vocabulary

Guess the word for the given definitions. Also form two sentences each using the word.

1. To stumble or fall
   _____

2. A poisonous reptile
   _____

3. A short swim
   _____

4. To collect or gather, or to scratch or scrape
   _____

5. To drink something by taking small mouthfuls
   _____

Write a sentence each using the words given below:

6. Rag :
   _____

   _____

   _____

   _____

7. Crush :

_____

_____

_____

8. Trash :

_____

_____

_____

9. Half :

_____

_____

_____

10. Table :

_____

_____

_____

_____

11. Matter :

_____

_____

_____

_____

12. Bet :

_____

_____

_____

13. Tent :

14. Held :

15. Else :

16. Health :

17. Measure :

18. Calm :

Grade 1
Volume 1
Week 6

19. Subtract :

20. Backpack :

21. Moose :

22. Army :

23. Weed :

SECTION 2 – Grammar

Fill in the blanks with appropriate vowels and learn the spellings:

1. R ____ V ____ R   (stream of water flowing into the sea)

2. M ____ ____NT ____ ____N   (a large steep hill)

3. CH ____ ____R   (a seat for one person)

4. W ____ ND ____ W   (an opening in the wall or vehicle fitted with glass)

5. L ____ ____F   (a quantity of bread)

Common Nouns: A common noun is a name given in general to every person or thing of the same class or kind.

Example: Foxes live in holes in the ground.

Example: The boy went to the market to buy oranges.

Abstract Nouns: A noun meaning an idea, quality, or state.

Example: Truth

Example: Danger

Collective Nouns: A count noun that means a group of individuals

Example: Family

Example: Crew

Material Nouns: A material or substance from which things are made

Example: Silver

Example: Plastic

List the common nouns in the following sentences and categorize them into abstract, collective, material nouns:

6. Cotton dresses are very cheap and comfortable.

_____

_____

7. My determination is to gain a higher education.

_____

8. Some animals move in herds.

_____

9. Weekends are a source of great joy for children.

_____

10. Members of this group are very active.

_____

11. My father owns a store of diamonds.

_____

_____

12. It is not true that a judge always gives the right justice.

_____

_____

13. There should be clarity to avoid any misunderstanding.

_____

_____

14. I bought a bunch of books.

_____

_____

15. Rain is one of the sources of water.

_____

_____

16. She was attacked by a swarm of wasps.

_____

_____

_____

17. I will surprise my mother as today is her birthday.

_____

_____

_____

SECTION 3 - Reading Comprehension

Read the passage and answer the questions given below:

Hummingbirds are the smallest non-extinct birds. They weigh less than a penny. They are barely more than two inches long.

They are known as hummingbirds because of the humming sound created by the flapping of their wings. Hummingbirds often appear in dazzling combinations of greens and reds or greens and blues. Others are violet, golden, orange, silver or other combinations. Hummingbirds are the only birds that can fly backwards.

Hummingbirds have long bills to insert into flowers to drink nectar. One can attract hummingbirds to their yard with special feeders filled with sugar water. Hummingbirds have a high metabolism to conserve energy when food is scarce. They are attracted to the color red.

Fill in the blanks with the right answers from the options given:
1. Hummingbirds are the only birds that _____
   A. Are small
   B. Will come to bird feeders
   C. Are green
   D. Can fly backwards

2. Compared to other birds, hummingbirds are _____
   A. About the same size
   B. Heavier
   C. Lighter
   D. Larger

3. Hummingbirds eat _____
   A. Flower nectar
   B. Berries
   C. The story doesn't say
   D. Insects

4. To attract hummingbirds to your yard, put feeders with _____ in them.
   A. Flowers
   B. Seeds
   C. Sugar water
   D. Berries

5. What color are most hummingbird feeders? _____
   A. Red
   B. Green
   C. White
   D. Golden

6. Write the definitions for the following words:

a. Extinct

_____

b. Flapping

_____

c. Dazzling

_____

d. Metabolism

_____

e. Feeders

_____

f. Conserve

_____

Read the poem given below and answer the following questions:

The Seed Shop

Here in a quiet and dusty room they lie,
Faded as crumbled stone or shifting sand,
Forlorn as ashes, shriveled, scentless, dry –
Meadows and gardens running through my hand.

On this brown husk a dale of hawthorn dreams,
A cedar in this narrow cell is thrust

That will drink deeply of century's streams,
These lilies shall make summer on my dust.

Here in their safe and simple house of death,
Sealed in their shells a million roses leap
Here I can blow a garden with my breath,
And in my hand a forest lies asleep.

- Muriel Stuart

7. What phrase does the speaker use to describe the room where the seeds are stored?

_____

_____

_____

8. When the cedar is planted, how long might it last?
   a. A day
   b. A year
   c. A decade
   d. A century

9. What phrases or words are used to describe the condition of the seeds?
   a. Slumbering
   b. Sweet-smelling
   c. Fresh
   d. Indestructible
   e. Stored temporarily
   f. Looking into the future
   g. Dead and gone

10. Write definitions for the following words and learn their spellings:

   a. Crumbled

   b. Forlorn
   _____

   c. Shriveled
   _____

   d. Cedar
   _____

   e. Thrust
   _____

   f. Dale
   _____

SECTION 4 – Writing

1. Describe the picture given below and write about it:

Image obtained from search engine^

2. Describe the picture given below and write about it:

Image obtained from search engine^

3. Going Green Challenge:

Donate your old toys, shoes and clothes instead of throwing them away. There are many kids who would be happy to receive them. Your old toys, shoes and clothes will make the needy kids happy.

Why? Charity is a good way to prove that love still exists. It gives people hope and belief in humanity. One of the most important to reasons to donate is that you can. Many of us were born more privileged than others. Use your privileges to bring hope to the underprivileged.

Week 6 - Puzzle 1 (Word Search)

Solve the following puzzle by finding all the hidden words!

```
A C E E D G O R E T S B T E F U R L R F L B
N L L E L T R S L L E A E C K T E D A M R E
E A Y E M L A C E L E C E A B R H D E E W R
U A M A E T A F E E K L N E A E S L E R R
R H A Y D A B T A T C P S K H S A R C L W D
E E E D T E C A U E A A C R A E L M M H T A
P B T E A E S R E H T C B E S L T T E B P A
R T M N E R B A T C P K T M T T H A R E H E
T A U B R R R A H Y R E M Y K T E E S R T A
Y B S L L H R Y A S R R T E T G H R F H E T
C K T T C A R T B U S E L N T N O A S L A D
H L E M A H G A S O C T E M S A P R E E M A
S T T R B H A A N A A T H O B E T H C T R G
L A L A A L E A R T R A T O S T L R M S T A
C E E C D M T M S A L M L S A E T E O L A S
B A A T R R Y O S F O R S E M T E S A T U T
A T C M M H K H L E M R K L D L A M A A T S
H R C T K R E E H B O S C L G E T A G B C T
R S B A A T P K E H L H M A L M B A S L T M
E C A E H R L B C E S G E P E R L D C E O P
R A D A C E N R E R S G A L M E D A A D H K
S S U A E S T E T E G C A E D E S A E M H E
```

Words List

moose	subtract	calm
held	bet	health
measure	crash	rag
matter	tent	else
army	half	TABLE
trash	weed	BACKPACK

Week 6 - Puzzle 2 (Word Scramble)

Unscramble the following list of shuffled words to meaningful words!

1. UASEEMR
2. FHLA
3. OSMOE
4. LDHE
5. RMAY
6. KCCPKBAA
7. ERMATT
8. LEHTHA
9. BTE
10. SARHT
11. TTNE
12. WEDE
13. SLEE
14. CLAM
15. RASCH
16. GRA
17. TELBA
18. TRTBCSUA

Grade 1
Volume 1
Week 7

Grade 1
Volume 1
Week 7

Teacher English Booklet

Level 1 - Week 7

Topics Covered Include:

Reading Comprehension
Writing
Vocabulary
Grammar

©All rights reserved-Math-Knots LLC., VA-USA   www.math-knots.com | www.a4ace.com

Grade 1
Volume 1
Week 7

SECTION 1 – Vocabulary

Guess the word for the given definitions. Also form two sentences each using the word.

1. A large area of water surrounded by land.

   _____

2. Stepping from one foot to the other with a hop or a bounce.

   _____

3. To emerge from sleep; stop sleeping.

   _____

4. A projection of the pelvis and the upper thigh bone on either side of a human body.

   _____

5. Forgery; imitation

   _____

Write 2 sentences each using the words given below:

6. Ink :

   _____

   _____

   _____

7. Zip:

8. Lift :

9. Built :

10. Silver :

11. Busy :

12. Hot :

Grade 1
Volume 1
Week 7

_____

13. Crop :

_____

_____

_____

_____

14. October :

_____

_____

_____

_____

15. Honest :

_____

_____

_____

16. Fought :

17. Caught:

18. Drawer :

19. Awful :

20. Jelly :

21. Ray:

22. Box :

23. Squeeze :

SECTION 2 – Grammar

List the common nouns in the following sentences and categorize them into abstract, collective, material nouns:

1. I really liked the group of dancers.

   _____

   _____

2. The condition of the poor people makes me sad.

   _____

   _____

3. I get new clothes every year for my birthday.

   _____

   _____

4. Helping others is a real source of joy.

   _____

   _____

5. The cheese is delicious.

   _____

   _____

Grade 1
Volume 1
Week 7

6. There is a huge library of books in my school.

_____

_____

7. I love my parents and grandparents as they take care of me.

_____

_____

8. Houses are made using bricks and cement.

_____

_____

9. I have a perfume.

_____

_____

10. There is a galaxy of stars in the sky.

_____

_____

11. Taking medicine gives me relief from infections.

_____

_____

SECTION 3 - Reading Comprehension

Read the passage and answer the questions given below:

Michael Phelps

Michael Phelps, the swimming champion, set a world record with 28 gold medals in the Olympics. He broke the record of the most decorated Olympian of all time during the Beijing Olympics in 2008 by winning eight gold medals. Michael Phelps surpassed the previously set record of seven gold medals by Mark Spitz.

Michael Phelps was born in Baltimore, Maryland in the United States. In the beginning Michael did not realize that his passion in life was to swim. In fact as a child, he was afraid of water. He tried his hands at various sports like soccer and baseball but gradually moved away from other sports and began training to be a swimmer under Coach Bob Bowman.

At the age of seven, Michael was diagnosed with ADHD (Attention Deficit Hyperactivity Disorder), a condition in which a child is constantly active and is unable to focus his/her attention on anything for even a short span of time. Michael found a release for this extra energy in swimming.

At school, he was bullied by his classmates for his big ears and lips. One of his teachers even told Michael's mother that he would never succeed at anything. Despite all odds, Michael's focus never changed, and he became what he dreamt of becoming – a real champion.

In the 2004 Olympics held at Athens, Greece, Michael won six gold and two bronze medals. During an interview after the Athens games, Michael recalls how he had trained for the games.

On cold, dark winter mornings when he did not feel like getting up to train at 5:30a.m., he would look inside his swimming cap. His cap had 'ATHENS' stitched on the inside. He focused on the words 'ATHENS'. It reminded him of his goal and he would grab his bag and head for the pool. He has been doing that ever since. He does not recall missing his training for anything – Christmas, New Year or Thanksgiving.

This young athlete spends most of his time training in the pool. Like most young people he is fond of movies and music. His favorite movie is Austin Powers and he loves video games and rap music. In one of his interviews he says that, "you should dream as big as possible because only then can you achieve your dream."

Michael studies tapes of his races repeatedly so that he doesn't repeat the same mistakes and can better his performance. He hates losing. Michael's determination and focused endeavor has made him a youth icon.

Answer the following questions:

1. How did Michael Phelps become interested in swimming?

_____

_____

_____

_____

_____

_____

_____

_____

_____

Grade 1
Volume 1
Week 7

2. What is ADHD?

_____

_____

_____

_____

_____

3. What 'odds' did Michael have to face in school?

_____

_____

_____

_____

_____

_____

4. How did Michael motivate himself to train for the 2004 Athens Olympics?

Grade 1
Volume 1
Week 7

5. What are Michael Phelp's other interests?

6. What message do we get from Michael's life?

7. What do you want to become when you grow up?

_____

_____

_____

_____

_____

_____

_____

_____

Write the words from the passage for the definitions given below:

8. Did better or improved upon

   _____

9. Detected

   _____

10. Period of time

    _____

11. To remember

    _____

12. Choose a sportsperson and prepare a brief outline about her/him. Use the given guidelines:

   a. The sportsperson's full name, age and nationality.
   b. Her/his appearance
   c. What she/he has done to become famous
   d. What is it that you like about her/him.
   e. Anything interesting or inspiring that you know about her/him.

   _____

   _____

   _____

_____

_____

_____

_____

_____

_____

13. Match the following:

1. Michael won eight gold medals at	a. ADHD
2. The previous record was set by	b. Austin Powers
3. He trained under the coach	c. The Athens Olympics
4. He was diagnosed with	d. Mark Spitz
5. He won six gold and two bronze medals at	e. The Beijing Olympics
6. Michael's favorite movie is	f. Bob Bowman

SECTION 4 – Writing

1. Describe the picture given below and write about it:

Image obtained from search engine^

2. Describe the picture given below and write about it:

Image obtained from search engine^

3. Going Green Challenge:

While purchasing products look for "recycled", "organic", "sustainably harvested" printed on the product and then purchase it.

Week 7 - Puzzle 1 (Word Search)

Solve the following puzzle by finding all the hidden words!

```
F I H R E T A V O R Z E F O H O O L E Y B O
A B L W E W S L F W W Y I H R L R T U H A U
E Y P B E P T E U H A A Z D E J B Z B L T L
Z B O N E S N U N K E S L F F O Z B G E T N
E O T X T C L D T O P B O W V R R I T Q O L
E L I T L T B Q T O H U S U B H G B Q R E E
U O T O T E W C R L G S D A E U O E L N T Y
Q D E C L A Z S I H I Y U O C C U B O O R B
S B E T P L I F T B U U P Z L O L I H Y E E
A C R O O L T I O H R H B S Y R G Q P I Z S
C T R B V T R H I R G I Y L O E Z T Z N Y L
P C F E T H T L P H F U H B H J E R E K Z I
A L R R O H R L I H D R A W E R V B C B L U
Y Q L Y L X U O R T T R H C Z H A U O C I S
T Y X I S E L E U O F L V C N Q U Y S A T G
Y O C V S E P L Z L L H S O I S E U H Y O I
B G U T K T O O O X T J R N A Z O A L E Z E
P O R I R C R G S E N F C L O S I W I E P Q
Z B O P E L V P L U O B T S O O A F O H H E
G R S R T O U R B N G E E Q N S J U Z A R T
B L U U H T Q T E I G Z I B J E L L Y V C T
J O T R U O O E A B L R X I H E H R Y F E E
```

Words List

INK	ZIP	LIFT
BUILT	SILVER	BUSY
HOT	CROP	OCTOBER
HONEST	FOUGHT	CAUGHT
DRAWER	AWFUL	JELLY
RAY	BOX	SQUEEZE

Week 7 - Puzzle 2 (Word Scramble)

Unscramble the following list of shuffled words to meaningful words!

1. UFGTOH
2. PZI
3. BLUTI
4. AYR
5. TOH
6. YLELJ
7. GHATUC
8. OXB
9. DRRWAE
10. SZUEEQE
11. LAWUF
12. FILT
13. CRPO
14. OEROTCB
15. SYBU
16. SVERLI
17. NOTHSE
18. IKN

Grade 1
Volume 1
Week 8

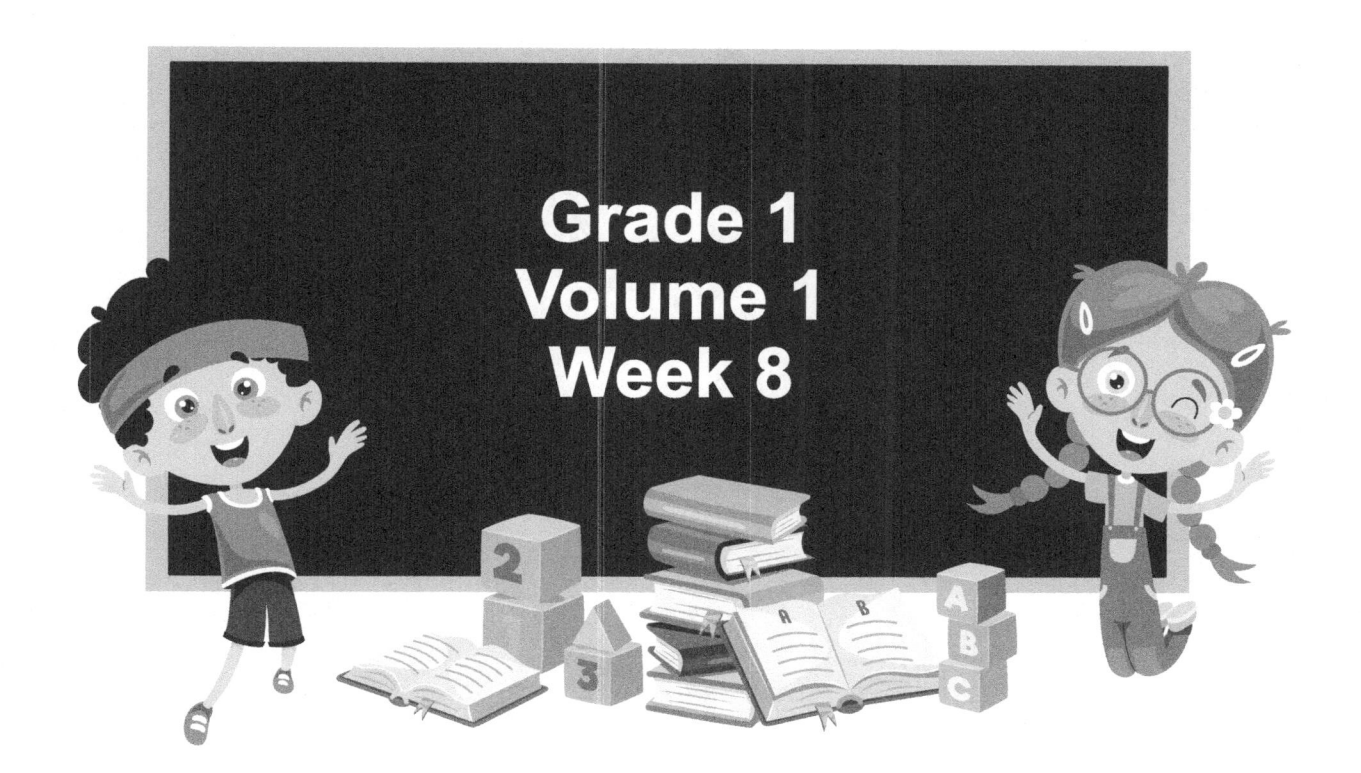

Teacher English Booklet

Level 1 - Week 8

Topics Covered Include:

**Reading Comprehension
Writing
Vocabulary
Grammar**

Grade 1
Volume 1
Week 8

SECTION 1 – Vocabulary

Write a sentence each using the words given below:

1. Pipe :

   _____

   _____

   _____

   _____

2. Mule :

   _____

   _____

   _____

   _____

3. Skate :

   _____

   _____

   _____

4. Care :

5. Size :

6. Wise:

7. Tiger :

8. Motor :

9. Student :

Grade 1
Volume 1
Week 8

10. Locate :

11. Lately:

12. Writer:

13. Thread :

14. Repeat :

15. Trunk :

16. Lily :

17. Pants :

18. Cheese:

Grade 1
Volume 1
Week 8

_____

_____

Write the meaning for each using the words given below:

19. Spun

_____

20. Glad

_____

21. Stun

_____

22. Fad

_____

23. Bun

_____

SECTION 2 – Grammar

Common Nouns: A common noun is a name given in general to every person or thing of the same class or kind.

Proper Nouns: A proper noun is a name of person, animal, place, or thing. Proper nouns begin with a capital letter.

Example: John
Example: Singapore

1. Column A gives a list of ten common nouns. Column B gives a list of ten proper nouns. Match them:

Column A	Column B
1. Country	a. White House
2. City	b. Barack Obama
3. Building	c. Bible
4. Leader	d. Japan
5. Car	e. New York
6. River	f. James
7. Book	g. Kate
8. Boy	h. Mt. Everest
9. Mountain Peak	i. Audi
10. Girl	j. Nile

Grade 1
Volume 1
Week 8

2. **Draw a circle around the common nouns and a line under the proper nouns:**

   a. The Alps is the highest mountain in Europe.

   b. The Nile is a very big river.

   c. New Delhi is the capital of India.

   d. The Pacific is the deepest ocean.

   e. Spiderman is a well-directed movie.

   f. Harry Potter is one of the most popular fiction books.

   g. January and February are the coldest months in the United States of America.

   h. Aladdin had a wonderful lamp.

   i. Pizza, burgers and French fries are all junk food.

   j. Sara and Zara work in an office in Virginia.

   k. Queen Elizabeth lives in Buckingham Palace in London.

3. Give a common noun for these proper nouns:

   a. Saturday, Thursday, Friday, Wednesday   _____

   b. Pacific, Atlantic, Indian   _____

   c. William Wordsworth, John Keats, W.B.Yeats   _____

   d. April, October, November, December   _____

SECTION 3 - Reading Comprehension

Read the passage and answer the questions given below:

Discovering Dinosaurs

Dinosaur remains have been found in all continents except Antarctica. The position of these sites depends on the age and type of the rocks, and a lucky discovery by a fossil collector! New dinosaur sites are discovered every year, and there are clearly many more to be found.

The first dinosaur remains were collected in the 19th century in England, often in old quarries, or at the foot of sea cliffs. Dinosaur fossils were soon discovered in other parts of Europe and North America. During the 20th century, large dinosaur collecting expeditions have gone to all corners of the world, and hundreds of huge bones have come to light.

Between 1895 and 1905, millionaire Andrew Carnegie, spent 25 million dollars on large fossil-collecting trips in Western America. A complete sk eleton of a Diplodocus was found for him in 1899, and Carnegie had a life-sized cast made and sent to all the leading museums in the world. One of his collectors, Earl Douglass, found a remarkable deposit of dinosaur skeletons in Colorado, and in 1925, was named the Dinosaur National Monument.

Similarly huge dinosaur deposits were discovered in the last century along the Red Deer River in Alberta, Canada. Barnum Brown and Charles Sternberg led two teams which collected hundreds of specimens between 1900 and 1920.

A huge dinosaur collecting expedition began in 1907 in Tanzania (then German East Africa). The German geologist, Werner Janensch, worked there for four years and sent 250 tons of bones back to Berlin, including those of the giant Brachiosaurus.

More recent finds have been made in Mongolia, China, Australia, South America and in 1988 in the Sahara Desert.

Complete the sentences by choosing the best ending:

1. Dinosaurs have been found all over the world except for
   _____.

   A. New Zealand
   B. Antarctica
   C. South America

2. The man who spent 25 million dollars looking for dinosaurs was
   _____.

   A. Barnum Brown
   B. Werner Janensch
   C. Andrew Carnegie

3. The complete skeleton Carnegie found was of _____.

   A. Diplodocus
   B. Brachiosaurus
   C. Triceratops

4. Brown and Sternberg collected dinosaur remains between
   _____.

   A. 1895 and 1905
   B. 1899 and 1915
   C. 1900 and 1920

5. The German geologist, Werner Janensch, worked in _____.

   A. Tanzania
   B. Colorado
   C. Alberta

6. Write the definitions for the following words:

   a. Continent

   _____

   b. Fossil

   _____

   c. Expedition

   _____

   d. Geologist

   _____

   e. Discovery

   _____

   f. Quarry

   _____

   g. Specimen

   _____

Grade 1
Volume 1
Week 8

Answer the following questions:

7. Why do you think some discoveries by fossil collectors are 'lucky'?

_____
_____
_____
_____
_____
_____
_____

8. Why do you think people keep looking for dinosaur fossils?

_____
_____
_____
_____

9. Research about any of the dinosaurs (Triceratops, Tyrannosaurus, Iguanadon, Stegosaurus) and try to find out the following:
   a. How long was it?
   b. How tall did it grow?
   c. What did it eat?
   d. Where in the world have its fossil been discovered?

_____

_____

_____

_____

_____

10. On the world map given below, find all the places where dinosaur fossils have been found. Write where the dinosaurs lived and the weather conditions they adapted to?

SECTION 4 – Writing

1. Describe the picture given below and write about it:

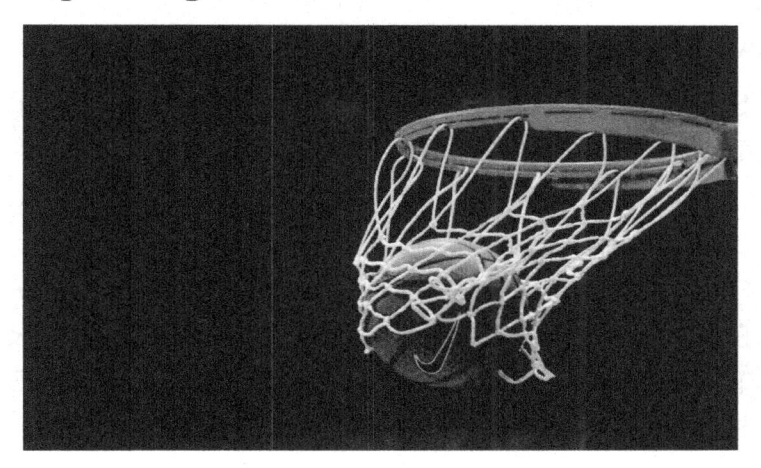

   Image obtained from search engine^

2. Describe the picture given below and write about it:

   Image obtained from search engine^

3. **Going Green Challenge:**

Make craft projects from recycled items such as can, carton boxes, or with your parents help create a rug using your old t-shirts.

Week 8 - Puzzle 1 (Word Search)

Solve the following puzzle by finding all the hidden words!

```
Z S E A W L L A S E E E E I T T C A C E E I
T Z Y S L S O P N I K O A P T H E H T I T D
E Z E T D T N I R R I A R N L R E T I R W E
P R S Y T T A I T G E Y R T R E G I T R T R
E O R U E R M E I I E I R T S A R E S Y R Z
S S E R C H U O S E E T S E P D L N M S T E
G T L E U S H N T D E E I S T P E N R M T S
N E R T N P W Z K L R E Z L I L Z H E E N T
R L M S M T I E A C A R E L R S I E E E D A
S T M N C M S P O Y I E R T D C L E E R R S
S A O E R W E T E E U E L L P R M E E E O E
R E T E O S E E E R Y T E U E E O E T E P E
H P R I L R P H R I O S T G E L I T E A S C
I E W N O N O E E Y E E H E N P A T N A E E
M R T T C T A I T E E H L L S K A T E O L K
C I O T A T D P T S P S Y E M M S O E Z K T
I M A A T T K A N T I L S M A R R E I L I I
L H M E E A U S E E E A E N N O E T E E Y A
T H M K E E R N D M M Y E D R T T U E E M A
A C M C L N D R U O P E R R S R R S Y I U E
E T W U Y L I L T I O S M L A E P E S P L E
R T M L E C P E S R K R E E I S T R A O I R
```

Words List

LOCATE	MOTOR	CARE
LATELY	THREAD	TRUNK
SIZE	CHEESE	PANTS
WRITER	TIGER	SKATE
PIPE	WISE	LILY
STUDENT	REPEAT	MULE

Week 8 - Puzzle 2 (Word Scramble)

Unscramble the following list of shuffled words to meaningful words!

1. ESUDTNT
2. LLYI
3. ZSIE
4. EECESH
5. WIRRTE
6. YTEALL
7. CREA
8. EIGTR
9. ESTKA
10. IPPE
11. PEREAT
12. TNSPA
13. EATHDR
14. LUEM
15. CEALOT
16. IESW
17. UTKNR
18. OORTM

Grade 1
Volume 1
Week 9

Grade 1
Volume 1
Week 9

Teacher English Booklet

Level 1 - Week 9

Topics Covered Include:

Reading Comprehension
Writing
Vocabulary
Grammar

SECTION 1 – Vocabulary

Write 2 sentences each using the words given below:

1. Than

   _____

   _____

2. Pot

   _____

   _____

3. Fan

   _____

   _____

4. Got

   _____

   _____

5. Van
_____

_____

Write a sentence each using the words given below:

6. April :
_____

_____

_____

_____

7. December :
_____

_____

_____

_____

8. November:
_____

9. Height :

10. Idea:

11. Able :

Grade 1
Volume 1
Week 9

12. June :

13. July :

14. May :

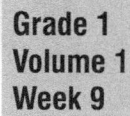

15. Break:

16. Library :

17. Knee :

18. Folks :

19. Halloween:

20. Camel :

21. Mess :

22. Boss :

23. Equivalent:

SECTION 2 – Grammar

Pronouns: It is a word used in place of a noun.

Compare the two sentences:

1. Elena is a nice girl. **Elena** is my cousin.
   Elena is a nice girl. **She** is my cousin.

Elena is a noun. **She** is a word used in place of this noun.

2. Alex: **I** like apples. **They** are good for health. **I** eat **them** every day.

Alex and **apples** are nouns. **I**, **they** and **them** are words used in place of these nouns.

1. **Underline the pronouns in the following sentences. Circle the nouns for which they stand:**

   a. Children should drink milk regularly. It is essential for growth.

   b. David and John studied the whole night. They had an examination the next day.

   c. Susan did not eat anything because she was not feeling well.

   d. Teacher: Did you participate in the quiz, Sam?
      Sam: Yes, ma'am. I won first prize.

   e. Carol had not done the work. Therefore, the teacher did not allow her to sit in the class.

   f. Stefan: This notebook is not yours, Rose.
      Rose: I know, it is not mine. I only want to see it.

   g. Teacher: Children, you must not eat too many sweets. They are not good for your health.

   h. Ellen: I know there are stars in the sky. But I cannot see them. Perhaps, they are behind the clouds.

2. Rewrite the sentences using pronouns in place of the nouns which are underlined.

a. This is Jack. <u>Jack</u> is a shopkeeper. All these shops are <u>Jack's</u>.

_____

_____

b. Ms. Anderson teaches us English. <u>Ms. Anderson</u> is very friendly with us. All of us like <u>Ms. Anderson</u> very much.

_____

_____

c. Katie and Tom are neighbors. <u>Katie and Tom</u> study in the same class. <u>Katie and Tom</u> go to school together. I am going to meet <u>Katie and Tom</u> in the evening.

_____

_____

d. Very few tigers are left in the world. We should try to protect <u>tigers</u>. We should never kill <u>tigers</u> for sport.

_____

_____

3. See the patterns and then fill in the blanks with the following words:
Mine / Ours / Yours / His / Hers / Theirs
Example: This is my notebook. The notebook is **mine**.

a. This is my car. This car is _____.

b. It was our gift. The gift was _____.

c. These are their notebooks. These notebooks are _____.

d. That is his school. That school is _____.

e. These are her crayons. These crayons are _____.

f. These are your shoes. These shoes are _____.

SECTION 3 - Reading Comprehension

Read the passage given below and answer the questions

Snakes

Snakes are reptiles. They have no legs but many ribs that help them to slide along the ground. They have no ears and no eyelids. Like all other reptiles, they are cold-blooded. Their temperature is controlled by their environment and they dislike very hot and very cold temperatures.

All snakes hunt. Poisonous snakes, such as cobras, poison their prey by biting them with their fangs. Constrictor snakes, such as pythons, coil themselves around their prey. Snakes that do not kill their prey by poison or constricting usually snatch it up and swallow it whole. Their mouths and jaws will stretch and open very wide.

There are nearly 2,500 different types of snakes in the world. Only 200 types of snakes are dangerous enough to kill people. The biggest, most deadly snake is the king cobra. The puff adder, which inhabits Africa, is also very dangerous.

Fill in the blanks with missing words:

1. Snakes move along the ground using their _____.

2. Snakes have no _____, no _____ and no _____.

3. Snakes _____ for their food.

4. There are 200 types of _____ snakes that can kill people.

5. The _____ lives in Africa.

Write the definitions for the following words:

6. Reptile

   _____

7. Environment

   _____

8. Prey

   _____

9. Fangs

   _____

10. Deadly

    _____

11. Inhabits

    _____

Answer the following questions:

12. What do all reptiles have in common?

_____

_____

_____

_____

13. How can some snakes swallow what they catch in one go. Research and write in detail?

_____

_____

_____

_____

14. Which is the biggest, deadliest snake? Research and write details about it?

15. Many people are frightened of snakes. Why do you think people are frightened?

_____

_____

_____

_____

16. Find an information book on snakes or go on the web. Choose one of the snakes given below:

    Grass Snake
    Boa constrictor
    Indian python
    Black Mamba

Answer the following questions and other information about the snake.

    A. How long does it grow?
_____

_____

_____

_____

_____

B. What does it feed on?

_____

_____

_____

_____

_____

C. Where does it live?

_____

_____

_____

_____

SECTION 4 – Writing

How to write informative essays?

1. The Beginning : It needs to introduce the topic and grab the attention of the reader.
2. The Subject or Middle : This is the main part of the entire essay. It will include important facts which will answer the reader's questions regarding the topic.
3. The Closing or Conclusion : This is where you will summarize your essay and spur the reader to learn more about the topic.

Write informative essays for the following topics:

1. The causes of Global Warming

2. How to buy a house?

3. **Going Green Challenge:**

   Use recyclable or waste products at home to create fabulous artwork. Research about all the artwork you can make from waste products and be creative while working on them.

Week 9 - Puzzle 1 (Word Search)

Solve the following puzzle by finding all the hidden words!

```
D E L L E E B R Y E S E I K E V O A L B I A
M S I E M Y K R H E B F U L E M S Y E Y A M
W F S A A E E S I M E R M Y L E K R U B E M
N O V E M B E R E O U L N Y M O Y H D L A M
O L D B M A R E E C S H E R R E E J U G J K
E K E E L A Y O Y V O E E B D I J E S A Y M
O S C E A W K H H S U R G S G L L U J Y H A
O E E E Y I O S K A E H E H U E B R L E E S
D S D L B L U B B J V E T A M R H O C J I N
R I F H Y C R Y O S E Y Y A B R N R U I R M
K H P I E A R L S A A J O S F L T N N J Y A
S S B E S L V A S S S L A C A R E E D E E L
L N O T B L R E B P O L E A H E E U I E R N
I L N E M D B E E R M E N M N N T L O A E S
C B C S D M H D R E E N I E E V K B A S B I
N E E A Y I B S I N D J B L E L B A B R O E
S Y B O R N N R K E E E N M W E C A E N S B
E L O N A I I M O E M R I A O O H L L R I R
J U K L R M E R M A B L E J L I B D M P B K
E J L E B I B D Y N M S N A L M G Y R S A I
C N Y S I R E D V I H E A E A B B E N R L Y
A L A E L I R P A H I V K B H E V M B D A L
```

Words List

ABLE	IDEA	JULY
NOVEMBER	JUNE	BOSS
LIBRARY	BREAK	HEIGHT
MESS	APRIL	DECEMBER
CAMEL	FOLKS	HALLOWEEN
MAY	KNEE	

Week 9 - Puzzle 2 (Word Scramble)

Unscramble the following list of shuffled words to meaningful words!

1. SSEM
2. YMA
3. CRMDEEBE
4. EVROMNBE
5. OSSB
6. BAEL
7. NJUE
8. KEEN
9. LIRPA
10. AIED
11. ENAHLEOLW
12. YLUJ
13. CAEML
14. ITEGHH
15. LAIRRYB
16. OFKLS
17. KREAB

Grade 1
Volume 1
Week 10

Grade 1
Volume 1
Week 10

Teacher English Booklet

Level 1 - Week 10

Topics Covered Include:

Reading Comprehension
Writing
Vocabulary
Grammar

Grade 1
Volume 1
Week 10

SECTION 1 – Vocabulary

Write a sentence each using the words given below:

1. January:

2. September :

3. February :

4. Happen :

5. Every :

6. Study :

Grade 1
Volume 1
Week 10

7. Dent :

8. Kettle :

9. Excellent :

10. Cent:

11. Ready:

Grade 1
Volume 1
Week 10

12. Heavy :

_____

_____

_____

_____

13. Glove :

_____

_____

_____

14. Cone :

_____

_____

_____

15. Snake :

16. Fairy :

17. Cloud :

18. Fault:

_____

_____

_____

_____

Guess the word for the given definitions. Also form two sentences each using the word.

19. A dark mark or stain made by ink, paint, or dirt.

_____

20. A golden-brown shade of skin developed by pale-skinned people after exposure to the sun.

_____

21. A particular place or point.

_____

22. To mark (letters, words, or other symbols) on a surface, typically paper, with a pen, pencil

_____

23. To write quickly

_____

Write the meanings for the following words:

24. Trigger

_____

25. Trap

_____

26. Bribe

_____

27. Digest

_____

28. Prey

_____

29. Enzymes

_____

30. Beneath

_____

31. Delicate

_____

SECTION 2 – Grammar

Underline the pronouns in the following sentences:

1. _____ should carry an umbrella as it is raining today.

2. _____ have gone to see the movie "Happy Feet".

3. _____ like mangoes but _____ sister likes grapes.

4. Mother told _____ to come home a little early today.

5. Anne and _____ are going for a picnic.

Fill in the blanks with suitable pronouns:

6. The teacher told _____ to open their books.

7. The dog limped because _____ had hurt its paw.

8. We looked for the lost dog. _____ could not find _____.

9. Let _____ go to the park.

10. Mickey Mouse is _____ favorite cartoon character.

11. David is a good boy. _____ always does _____ work on time. All the teachers like _____.

12. I have a book. _____ is very interesting. _____ had many pictures of dolphins. I like _____ very much.

13. Where is Sheila? Oh! It's late again. _____ told _____ to come on time today.

14. The boys helped the old man. _____ thanked

_____.

15. The students had worked hard for _____ play.

_____ came first. The teachers praised

_____.

Kinds of Pronouns:

1. **Personal Pronouns:** Personal pronouns stand for three Persons: 1st person, 2nd person and 3rd person.

   Example:
   a. The pronouns which refer to the person or persons speaking are called Pronouns of the First Person, that is – I, we, mine, us, mine, ours.
   b. The pronouns which refer to the person or people spoken to are called Pronouns of the Second Person, that is – you, yours.
   c. The pronouns which refer to the person or things spoken of are called Pronouns of the Third Person, that is – he, she, him, her, they, them, their, it.

Fill in the blanks with Personal Pronouns:

16. Ms. Simpsons is ill. _____ is on medicines.

17. Tell those girls that _____ must go.

18. Has Mr. Adams gone? _____ think this bag is _____.

19. _____ am sorry if _____ have hurt _____.

20. Is this your bag or _____ mine_____?

2. **Reflexive Pronouns:** The pronouns such as – myself, yourself, himself, herself, itself, themselves, behave like Objects to Verbs, but they refer to the same person as the subjects to the verbs. These pronouns are called Reflexive Pronouns.

Fill in the blanks with Reflexive Pronouns:

21. The old man often talks to _____.

22. Have you looked at _____ lately in the mirror?

23. Marie does all her household chores _____.

24. The horse has hurt _____.

25. I enjoyed _____ when I went to Egypt.

26. The sons fought amongst _____ after the death of their father.

27. The old lady looked after _____ as she lived alone.

3. **Possessive Pronouns:** Possessive pronouns are those that indicate Possession or Relationship.
Example: mine, ours, yours, his, hers, its, theirs.

Fill in the blanks with Possessive Pronouns:

28. I own that kitten. It is _____.

29. He owns that horse. It is _____.

30. You own that car. It is _____.

31. She owns that i-pod. It is _____.

32. We own that farm. It is _____.

33. They own that factory. It is _____.

4. **Demonstrative Pronouns:** This, these, that, those are used to point out the objects. This and these refer to things near at hand. That and those refer to things at a distance. They are called Demonstrative Pronouns.

Fill in the blanks with demonstrative pronouns:

34. _____ is Ashley's car.

35. _____ are Mr. Brown's dogs.

36. _____ is my video camera. _____ is yours.

37. _____ are ripe bananas, _____ are unique.

38. _____ cat is white, but _____ is black.

39. _____ is Glen's pen. _____ is yours.

5. **Interrogative Pronouns:** Pronouns such as who, what, which, whom are used for asking questions. Pronouns used for asking questions are called interrogative pronouns.

Fill in the blanks with interrogative pronouns:

40. _____ is the news?

41. _____ do you want to see?

42. _____ did you give my ball to?

43. _____ broke the play station?

44. _____ is your brother's i-pod?

45.

SECTION 3 - Reading Comprehension

Read the passage given below and answer the questions:

The Sloth

Did you know that there is an animal which spends all its time hanging upside down, and most of its life asleep?

This animal is the sloth. The sloth is a mammal, which feeds on its mother's milk when young. It is found in the jungles of South America and is one of the laziest animals alive! It eats and sleeps upside down, holding on to the branch of a tree with its toes; it moves from a place only when it has finished eating all the food nearby.

It stays without moving for such a long time to hide from its enemies. Dangerous animals, which might otherwise kill it leave it alone. As they go by beneath a tree, they do not notice the sloth which is hanging from the branches.

The word 'sloth' is now a part of the English Language. To be 'slothful' is to be 'lazy', like the sloth.

Read the sentences and fill in the blanks with the right word from the list of words given below:

South America / place / mammal / lazy / see

1. The sloth is a _____.

2. It is found in the jungles of _____.

3. It stays in one _____ till it has finished all the food nearby.

4. Its enemies do not kill it because they do not _____ it.

5. Slothful means _____.

Read the sentences and fill in the blanks with the right word from the list of words given below:

Spends / stays / alone / held / asleep

6. The child _____ her mother's hand as they crossed the road.

7. Max _____ every Sunday playing cricket.

8. He was tired and fell _____ as soon as he lay down.

9. The rich man _____ in the best hotel when he goes to Brazil.

10. Sheila was _____ in the house because her mother had gone shopping.

Read the story given below and answer the following questions:

In this story by Robin Bloksberg, Elena, and her family move to America. Read how Elena makes new friends and adjusts to her new life.

When Elena was little, she lived in Russia. Russia is a very big country. Even so, Elena's own world was small. All she knew was the little village where she and her family lived. Then when Elena was nine, her father told her, "Elena, we're moving to America." When Elena's family first arrived in America, they stayed with her uncle in Evanston, Illinois. Evanston looked nothing like Russia. Elena felt very shy when she went into town. The people looked different from the people she knew in Russia. Everything seems strange. Elena felt like a stranger. Being a stranger was no fun.

When Elena's father started his new job, they had to move to Chicago. Elena spent the rest of the summer exploring the city with her mother and sister. When they spoke Russian to each other, people would sometimes stare. It was not easy getting used to a new home. In Russia, Elena had lived in a little town. There were few people. She knew everyone. Here, there were so many people! Elena and her family didn't know anyone. Elena wasn't sure she would be happy in America.

In September, Elena started school. She was nervous. There were other children at school from different countries. A boy names Ivan was also from Russia. It felt wonderful for Elena to talk to him in Russian. At Elena's school in Russia, she had lots of friends. At her new school, Elena knew only Evan at first.

Ivan was a good friend, but sometimes Elena missed having girlfriends. Then she tried out for the basketball team. She was very proud when she qualified for the team! She was even happier when the team members hugged her. Some of the girls on the basketball team became her good friends. When she made mistakes in English, they helped her learn to say things the right way. As Elena's English got better, it was easier to make new friends. Some of the girls invited her to see a movie. Elena had not laughed so much since she had left Russia. She understood most of it, too!

Sometimes Elena has dreams about Russia, her beautiful country. She can still picture the river that ran through the town where she lived. She can remember the taste of the salted fish she loved so well. Elena will always be a Russian. But she is also starting to feel like an American. Elena feels as if she has two homes – the one she left behind and the beautiful one that she now loves.

Choose the correct answers for the following questions:

11. Where did Elena live when she was little?
    A. Russia
    B. America
    C. Illinois
    D. Evanston

12. Why did Elena feel shy when she went into town in America?
    A. Because Evanston was not like Russia.
    B. Because people were rude.
    C. Because her mother spoke to her in Russian.
    D. Because she felt like a stranger.

13. According to Elena, what was the biggest difference between her town in Russia and the city in Chicago?
    A. The people in Chicago did not speak Russian.
    B. There were few people in Russia, but so many in Chicago.
    C. She had a lot of friends in Russia.
    D. The house in Chicago was uncomfortable.

14. When did it become easier for Elena to make new friends?
    A. When she made friends with Ivan.
    B. When she tried out for the basketball team.
    C. When her English got better.
    D. When she was invited to a movie.

15. How did Elena finally feel about America?
    A. She did not like it because there was no salted fish here.
    B. She liked it better than Russia because she had new friends now.
    C. She was confused about her feelings towards her new home.
    D. It had become her second home and she had started to love it.

SECTION 4 – Writing

Write informative essays for the following topic:

1. Causes and Consequences of a War.

2. Going Green Challenge:
   Make a family tree using the leaves fallen on the ground and add it to your art book. Be as creative as you can.

Week 10 - Puzzle 1 (Word Search)

Solve the following puzzle by finding all the hidden words!

```
O Y E E Y R E A A E E Y N E K S D P K K F V
T T T D S B U E U L S S E Y D R R L T H P X
Y A U L S S U L D E E T R Y R S E Y E A B T
H V A N A A E U P B P N O A T E Y A D E T R
P F L E B L N T N E C F N A I D V T L N E L
V E I E A P E E J B L A T Y E Y U E H E U E
O Y S A N M R N K T T S H A R H A P P E N R
E E E Y B R O O N A C R E D E J T F L O D U
L N T E A F L C S R N U A X A L O E E L V C
T V R R L E E E O T V S C V D T T V R Y C F
Y D O G U E D Y E E U E R O Y A I T E V I E
Y D R L D T E T T R L D L E L B E E E S S I
T E G O R D F A U L T E Y E A L I H T K F N
E V O V H T U F E B R U A R Y T A T E V A Y
O E P E P L N N E N J A N U A R Y S N E A Y
F Y A R R N T R D H D U O L C Y I L N E D R
V T U N I T N E F G T A F P J U E A Y Y D L
V Y R E R T P S H P I O Y Y L N Y T F E P V
D Y E R E R I D U Y R P V D A E E S L J A E
N A A E N R E U G U L U D L N H R E A C T B
P E E E Y O P N U H U E E N Y T F U E T E E
A E R U L X R S X D N U P A R Y U T N R A E
```

Words List

SNAKE	STUDY	FEBRUARY
EXCELLENT	SEPTEMBER	FAULT
CONE	CENT	HAPPEN
READY	KETTLE	FAIRY
JANUARY	EVERY	HEAVY
GLOVE	DENT	CLOUD

Week 10 - Puzzle 2 (Word Scramble)

Unscramble the following list of shuffled words to meaningful words!

1. CEELLXNET
2. MRBTSPEEE
3. AEKSN
4. NEDT
5. ENCT
6. EHYAV
7. AFTUL
8. IRFAY
9. LTKETE
10. OLCDU
11. VLGOE
12. TDYSU
13. OECN
14. REYVE
15. RDYAE
16. EHPANP
17. FRYUAERB
18. JANYRUA

Grade 1
Volume 1
Answer Keys

Grade 1
Volume 1
Ans Keys

WEEK 1 : SECTION 1 – Vocabulary

1 - 24: Answers vary

SECTION 2 – Grammar

1.
- A. S
- B. Q
- C. C
- D. C
- E. S
- F. Q
- G. Q
- H. C
- I. C
- J. S
- K. S
- L. Q
- M. C
- N. C
- O. Q

2 – 25) Answers vary

SECTION 3 - Reading Comprehension

1.

a. It is difficult for ostriches to fly because they are very big. Instead of flying, they run. They have very powerful legs and can run almost as fast as a horse.

b. Ostriches live in the dry parts of Africa. They usually eat plants, but water & sometimes they eat small reptiles. They can even go for a long time without water if they have enough green plants to eat.

c. When scared, the Ostrich will either hide themselves by lying flat against the ground or run away.

d. When cornered, the Ostriches can attack with the kick of its powerful legs.

2.
   a. True
   b. False
   c. True

3.
   a. Having great strength
   b. Take aggressive action against
   c. Relatively great size, extent, or capacity
   d. Unable to exist or occur

4. Answers vary

5.
   a. Answers vary
   b. Strawberry flavors are also widely used in many products like lip gloss, candy, perfume, and many others. They are also used in desserts, milkshakes, and other food products.
   c. Strawberry is the only fruit that has seed on the outside and there are about 200 seeds in each strawberry.
   d. The first strawberry was grown in Brittany in France. The strawberry museum is in Belgium.

6. Answers vary

7. Answers vary

8.
   a. The worth or usefulness of something
   b. Habitually done, used, or found
   c. A building in which objects of historical, scientific, artistic, or cultural interest are stored and exhibited
   d. A substance or plant having healing properties.

9.
   a. False
   b. True
   c. True
   d. False
   e. False

WEEK 2 : SECTION 1 – Vocabulary

1-18: Answers vary

SECTION 2 – Grammar

1-21: Answers vary

22. Make the following sentences negative:

   a. His memory is not sharp
   b. My school is not far from my house.
   c. Do not/Don't water these plants daily.
   d. Do not/Don't write fast.
   e. The dog is not barking loudly.
   f. It is not humid today.
   g. My mother is not at home today.
   h. We cannot stand and talk here.
   i. The river was not deep.
   j. She did not have a beautiful dress.
   k. Do not/Don't leave the room.
   l. I should not see him.
   m. They have not arrived.
   n. We do not have a holiday today.
   o. Do not/Don't sit down.
   p. He will not leave today.
   q. I am not happy.
   r. Peter cannot run fast.

s. These questions are not difficult.
t. All these cars are not for sale.

SECTION 3 - Reading Comprehension

1. Answer the following:

   a. In olden times, people used smoke signals, pigeons, horses, and mail runners to send messages from one place to another.

   b. Old means of communication: Slow – Sometimes messages never reached the destination. New means of communication:
   Fast – Easy – Low in cost compared to old mean of communication.

   c. Graham Bell invented the photophone.

   d. The older means of communication took a lot of time to deliver messages. If something happened to the pigeons, horses or mail runners, the messages would never reach their destination. Smoke signals were used to alert soldiers of danger but could create chaos if lit in the wrong way.

   e. The first telephone did not have a bell. The caller had to tap the phone with a hammer. That way, the receiver at the other end, would know that there was an incoming call.

   f. Answers vary

2.
   a. False
   b. False
   c. False
   d. False

3.
   a. Means of sending and receiving information
   b. The place to which someone or something is to be sent.
   c. Confusion and disorder
   d. A person who has expert knowledge in natural or physical sciences.
   e. A person who has invented a particular process or device.

f. A thing invented for a particular purpose

g. To pass something from one person or place to another.

4-6) Answers vary

SECTION 4 – Writing

Answers vary

WEEK 3 : SECTION 1 – Vocabulary

1-18) Answers vary

SECTION 2 – Grammar

1.

    a. I have no money in my purse.

    b. Do not/Don't sit in the open.

    c. He is not speaking the truth.

    d. I had not kept those chocolates for you.

    e. I will not go the market tomorrow.

    f. Do not/Don't give me milk and bread.

    g. Do not/Don't close the windows.

    h. She is not writing neatly.

2.

    a. Are we late?

    b. Is she old?

    c. Was the sound clear?

    d. Were his clothes dirty?

    e. Had she had a watch?

    f. Have they seen the White House?

    g. Will he leave early?

h.   Is the meeting at 6pm?

i.   Is the road to the station narrow and bumpy?

j.   Has she two sisters?

k.   Will she be rewarded for her honesty?

l.   Should you believe him?

m.   Are the boys reading books?

n.   Was that snake dangerous?

o.   Is my sister very fond of music?

p.   Can he drive a car?

q.   Is the telephone bell ringing?

r.   Are these diamonds real?

s.   Were the workers faithful to the company?

t.   Is somebody knocking at the door?

SECTION 3 - Reading Comprehension

1.

   a. When Helen Keller was just two-year-old she had become blind and deaf. Her world turned dark, silent, lonely, and very sad. But she overcame her obstacles and went to college, wrote books, and did a lot of work to help the blind and the deaf. When she was sixteen, she spoke five different languages. This made her different from others.

   a. Ms. Sullivan taught Helen to read and write in Braille. Braille has worked patterns of raised dots that can be felt with fingertips. Teacher and pupil very hard. Neither teaching nor learning was easy.

   b. Beethoven is the greatest musician of all times. He began to lose his loss hearing at an early age and become totally deaf at the age of 44. But the of hearing did not stop him from composing and playing music for people to enjoy. Beethoven's passion for music makes his music special.

c. Stephen Hawking is the greatest physicist in the world. He has a rare and disability that has paralyzed him over these years. But he did not give up he achieved great success in the field of physics. He has won many awards including the Presidential Medal of Freedom.

2. Answers vary

3.
- a. A repeated decorative design
- b. To write or create (art – music or poetry)
- c. A physical or mental condition that limits a person activity, senses or movement.
- d. Cause a person or part of a body to become incapable of movement.

4.
- a. Pollution causes harm to the entire ecosystem. It causes direct impact on the health of humans and animals. Breathing polluted air puts you at a higher risk for respiratory diseases. Fishes living in polluted water may die due to chemicals and other substances. Drinking polluted water causes diarrhea and other harmful diseases.
- b. Plants help in cleaning the polluted air. Plants also help to lessen noises around us. For each tree we cut, three more should be planted.
- c. Answers vary

5.
- a. dirty
- b. mother cares
- c. fertile
- d. ecosystem
- e. spaces

6.
- a. Tiger
- b. Rhinoceros
- c. Giant Panda
- d. Duck
- e. Wolf
- f. Elephant
- g. Penguin

7. Answers vary

SECTION 4 – Writing

Answers vary

WEEK 4 : SECTION 1 – Vocabulary

1-18: Answers Vary

SECTION 2 – Grammar

1.
- a. Will Sara come tomorrow?
- b. Will Anthony win the competition?
- c. Had the bulls managed to escape?
- d. Have they climbed the mountain together?
- e. Is Brad crossing the street

2. Answers vary

3.
e
a
o
i
u
e
o

**Grade 1
Volume 1
Ans Keys**

4. Mark the consonants only:

d
c
j
x
v
p
g

5.

a. P A RR O T

b. Q U E E N

c. B U TT E R

d. L A PT O P

e. H O RS E

f. C O MP A SS

g. T E L E PH O N E

h. C A B

6.

a. A PPL E   (a fruit)

b. U MBR E LL A   (we use it during rain)

c. F I NG E R   (part of our body)

d. P I G E O N   (a bird)

e. SCH OO L   (we go here to study)

f. SH O E S   (We wear them on our feet)

7.

a. O N IO N   (a vegetable)

b. P I N EA P P L E   (a juicy fruit)

c. P E A C O C K (a colorful bird)

d. C A K E (birthdays are incomplete without eating this)

e. G UI T A R (a musical instrument)

f. S P OO N (we use it to eat our meals)

SECTION 3 - Reading Comprehension

1. Answers vary
2. Answers vary
3. Plastic particles from water bottles and cosmetics will pollute the water.   Plastics are also non-biodegradable substances i.e., they are harmful to the nature. Hence, it is always suggested to recycle plastics.
4. Answers vary
5.
   a. schools / restaurants,
   b. recycling center.
   c. cleaned / plastic / color
   d. shredding
   e. flakes
6.
   a. Huge or gigantic
   b. Presence of a harmful substance in the environment.
   c. A biological community of interacting physical components
   d. Throw away
   e. Organized or arranged
   f. Substances with disturbs the purity of something.
   g. To tear or cut (paper, cloth, or food)

7. Answers Vary

   a. Burning strongly or has the bright color of fire.

   b. Make a continuous rattling sound.

   c. Quickly or promptly.

   d. Flow out of something in the form of a rapid stream.

e. Sound of heavy footsteps.

f. A pointy part of the foot, especially of a horse.

SECTION 4 – Writing

Answers vary

WEEK 5 : SECTION 1 – Vocabulary

1. phone

2. Buck

3. Bug

4. Grip

5. Cake

6 – 23) Answers Vary

SECTION 2 – Grammar

1.
> u
> e
> o
> i
> a
> i
> a

2.
  a. C <u>U</u> P (we use this to drink tea or coffee)

  b. <u>I</u> GL <u>O O</u> (home of Eskimos)

  c. <u>O</u> CT <u>O</u> P <u>U</u> S (a water animal with many tentacles)

  d. D <u>AI</u> SY (a flower)

  e. SH <u>E E</u> P (this animal gives us wool)

f. F I R E   (this element causes burns)

g. B A TT E RY   (a portable energy supplier)

3.

a. M I C R O W A V E   (used to warm food)

b. I C E C R EA M   (a dessert that is served cold)

c. S T AI R C A S E   (used to move from one floor to another)

d. S U P E R H E R OE S   (Superman, Batman and the Avengers are called this)

e. E L E PH A N T   (A large grey animal with a trunk)

f. K E Y   (Used to open locked doors)

g. F A M I L Y   (The people closest to you. You live with them)

SECTION 3 - Reading Comprehension

1.

a. Malala Yousafzai is a Pakistani activist for women education and human rights. She is the youngest Nobel Prize winner. She founded the Malala fund, a non-profit organization working towards the education for women.

b. Malala was awarded a Nobel Peace Prize for her struggle against the suppression of children and young people and for the right of all children education.

c. Answers vary

d. Answers vary

2.

a. A person who campaigns to bring about a social or political change.

b. Regularly updated web page written in an informal manner.

c. Job or profession

d. Based on official documents or actual events (interviews)

e. Take part in something to prevent a result of events.

f. To stop an activity or publication

g. A firm determination to do something

h. A person forced to leave the country as a result of war or disaster

i. To prevent someone from doing something.

j. To make an effort to achieve something.

3. Answers Vary

4.
    a. True

    b. False

    c. False

    d. True

    e. True

5. a.

6. b

7. c

8. c

9. The third stanza of the poem states: "Chairs to mend, and delft to sell!"

   This line indicates that the pedlar was able to mend things.

10.

    a. A vehicle equipped with living –in facilities.

    b. A person who goes from place to place selling small goods.

    c. A pipe which conducts smoke from a fire.

    d. Tin-glazed earthenware.

SECTION 4 – Writing

Answers vary

WEEK 6 : SECTION 1 – Vocabulary

1. Trip

2. Snake

3. Dip

4. Rake

5. Sip

6 – 23) Answers Vary

SECTION 2 – Grammar

1. R I V E R   (stream of water flowing into the sea)
2. M O U NT A I N   (a large steep hill)
3. CH A I R   (a seat for one person)
4. W I ND O W   (an opening in the wall or vehicle fitted with glass)
5. L O A F   (a quantity of bread)
6. Cotton – Material noun . Cheap, Comfortable – Abstract nouns.
7. Determination, education – Abstract noun.
8. Herd – Collective noun
9. Joy – Abstract noun. Children – Collective noun
10. Members – Collective noun. Active – Abstract noun.
11. Diamonds – Material noun
12. Justice – Abstract noun

13. Clarity – Abstract noun
14. Bunch – Collective noun

15. Water – Material noun

16. Attacked – Abstract noun

    Swarm – Collective noun

    Wasps – Material noun

17. Surprise – Abstract noun

SECTION 3 - Reading Comprehension

1. D

2. C

3. A

4. C

5. A

6.
    a. Having no living members.

    b. Wings of a bird move up and down while flying.

    c. Extremely bright to blind the eyes temporarily.

    d. A chemical process that occurs in a living organism to maintain life.

    e. A container filled with food for birds or mammals.

    f. Protect something from harm or destruction.

7. First line of the first stanza: "Here in a quiet and dusty room they lie"

8. d

9. g

10.
  a. Break or fall apart into small fragments

  b. Abandoned or lonely.

  c. Wrinkled due to loss of moisture.

  d. Conifers which yield fragrant, durable timber.

  e. Force or to push suddenly in a specific direction.

  f. A valley

SECTION 4 – Writing

Answers vary

WEEK 7 : SECTION 1 – Vocabulary

1. Lake

2. Skip

3. Wake

4. Hip

5. Fake

6 – 23) Answers vary

SECTION 2 – Grammar

1. Group – Collective noun

   Liked – Abstract noun

2. Poor, sad – Abstract nouns

3. New – Abstract noun

   Clothes – Material noun

4. Helping, Joy – Abstract nouns

5. Cheese - Material noun

   Delicious – Abstract noun

6. Huge – Abstract noun

   Library, school – Collective nouns.

7. Love, care – Abstract nouns.

8. Houses, bricks, cement – Material nouns

9. Perfume – Material noun

10. Galaxy – Collective noun

11. Medicine – Material noun

    Relief – Abstract noun

SECTION 3 - Reading Comprehension

1. As a child, Phelps was afraid of water. He tried his hands at various sports like soccer and baseball but gradually moved away from other sports and began training to be a swimmer under coach Bob Bowman.

2. Attention Deficit Hyperactivity Disorder, a condition in which a child is constantly active and is unable to focus his/her attention on anything for even a short span of time.

3. At school, Phelps was bullied by his classmates for his big ears and lips. One of his teachers even told Michael's mother that he would never succeed at anything.

4. Before the Athens Olympics, during cold, dark winter mornings when his on Phelps did not feel like getting up to train at 5:30a.m., he would look inside swimming cap. His cap had 'ATHENS' stitched on the

inside. He focused the words 'ATHENS'. It reminded him of his goal and he would grab his bag and head for the pool.

5. Michael Phelps is fond of movies and music. His favorite movie is Austin Powers and he loves video games and rap music.

6. Answers vary

7. Answers vary

8. Surpassed

9. Diagnosed

10. Span

11. Recall

12. Answers vary

13.

1. Michael won eight gold medals at	a. ADHD (4)
2. The previous record was set by	b. Austin Powers (6)
3. He trained under the coach	c. The Athens Olympics (5)
4. He was diagnosed with	d. Mark Spitz (2)
5. He won six gold and two bronze medals at	e. The Beijing Olympics (1)
6. Michael's favorite movie is	f. Bob Bowman (3)

SECTION 4 – Writing

Answers vary

WEEK 8 : SECTION 1 – Vocabulary

1-18) Answers vary

19. Turn or whirl around quickly. 2. Skip

20. Happy

21. Astonish or shock so that they are temporarily unable to react.

22. Short-lived enthusiasm

23. A small cake containing dry fruits.

SECTION 2 – Grammar

1.

Column A	Column B
1. Country	a. White House (3)
2. City	b. Barack Obama (4)
3. Building	c. Bible (7)
4. Leader	d. Japan (1)
5. Car	e. New York (2)
6. River	f. James (8)
7. Book	g. Kate (10)
8. Boy	h. Mt. Everest (9)
9. Mountain Peak	i. Audi (5)
10. Girl	j. Nile (6)

2. **Draw a circle around the common nouns and a line under the proper nouns:**

   a. The Alps is the highest **mountain** in Europe.

   b. The Nile is a very big **river**.

   c. New Delhi is the capital of India.

   d. The Pacific is the deepest **ocean.**

   e. Spiderman is a well-directed **movie**.

   f. Harry Potter is one of the most popular fiction **books**.

   g. January and February are the coldest **months** in the United States of America.

   h. Aladdin had a wonderful lamp.

   i. Pizza, burgers and French fries are all junk **food**.

   j. Sara and Zara work in an office in Virginia.

   k. Queen Elizabeth lives in Buckingham Palace in London.

3. Give a common noun for these proper nouns:

   a. Weekdays

   b. Ocean

   c. Poets

   d. Months

SECTION 3 - Reading Comprehension

1. B
2. C
3. A
4. C
5. A
6.

    a. large area of land (Example: Asia, Europe, Africa, etc)

    b. The remains or impressions of a plant or animal embedded in a rock.

    c. A journey undertaken by a group of people to go to a place.

    d. An expert or student of geology.

    e. The action of disclosure or being discovered.

    f. A large pit from which stone or other materials must be extracted.

    g. An individual plant, animal, or piece of a mineral.

7 – 10) Answers vary

SECTION 4 – Writing

Answers vary

WEEK 9 : SECTION 1 – Vocabulary

1-23) Answers vary

SECTION 2 – Grammar

1. **Bold words are nouns in the below**

    a. Children should drink **milk** regularly. <u>It</u> is essential for growth.

    b. **David** and **John** studied the whole night. <u>They</u> had an examination the next day.

    c. **Susan** did not eat anything because <u>she</u> was not feeling well.

    d. Teacher: Did <u>you</u> participate in the quiz, Sam?
       Sam: Yes, ma'am. <u>I</u> won first prize.

    e. **Carol** had not done the work. Therefore, the teacher did not allow <u>her</u> to sit in the class.

    f. Stefen: This notebook is not <u>yours</u>, Rose.
       Rose: <u>I</u> know, it is not <u>mine</u>. <u>I</u> only want to see it.

    g. Teacher: Children, you must not eat too many **sweets**. <u>They</u> are not good for your health.

    h. **Ellen**: <u>I</u> know there are **stars** in the sky. But <u>I</u> cannot see <u>them</u>. Perhaps, <u>they</u> are behind the clouds.

2.

    a. This is Jack. He is a shopkeeper. All these shops are his.

    b. Ms. Anderson teaches us English. She is very friendly with us.

       All of us like her very much.

    c. Katie and Tom are neighbors. They study in the same class.

       They go to school together. I am going to meet them in the evening.

    d. Very few tigers are left in the world. We should try to protect them.

       We should never kill them for sport.

3.
   a. mine.
   b. ours.
   c. theirs.
   d. his.
   e. hers.
   f. yours.

SECTION 3 - Reading Comprehension

1. Snakes move along the ground using their ribs.
2. Snakes have no legs, no ears and no eyelids.
3. Snakes hunt for their food.
4. There are 200 types of poisonous snakes that can kill people.
5. The King Cobra lives in Africa.
6. A vertebrate animal. (Snakes, lizards, crocodiles, turtles, and tortoises)
7. The surrounding in which a person, plant or animal lives and operates.
8. An animal that is hunted and killed by another for food.
9. Sharp, grooved teeth of the venomous snake.
10. Able to cause death
11. Live in or occupy
12. All reptiles are cold-blooded. Their very temperature is controlled by their environment and they dislike very hot and cold temperatures.
13 - 16) Answers Vary

SECTION 4 – Writing

Answers vary

WEEK 10 : SECTION 1 – Vocabulary

1-18) Answers Vary

19. Blot

20. Tan

21. Spot

22. Write

23. Jot

24. Response to a particular action, process, or situation.

25. A device used to catch and retain animals.

26. Persuade someone to act in one's favour.

27. Breakdown the food into substances that can be absorbed by the body.

28. An animal that is hunted and killed by another for food.

29. A substance produced by the body which acts as a catalyst to a biochemical reaction.

30. Underneath or a level lower

31. Easily broken or fragile

SECTION 2 – Grammar

1. <u>You</u> should carry an umbrella as it is raining today.
2. <u>They</u> have gone to see the movie "Happy Feet".

3. <u>I</u> like mangoes but <u>my</u> sister likes grapes.
4. Mother told <u>us</u> to come home a little early today.
5. Anne and <u>I</u> are going for a picnic.

6. them

7. it

8. we / it

9. us

10. my

11. He / his / him

12. It / It

13. I / her

14. He / them

15. their / They / them

16. Ms. Simpsons is ill. She is on medicines.

17. Tell those girls that they must go.

18. Has Mr. Adams gone? I think this bag is his.

19. I am sorry if I have hurt you.

20. Is this your bag or mine ?

21. himself

22. yourself

23. herself

24. itself

25. myself

26. themselves

27. herself

28. mine

29. his

30. yours

31. hers

32. ours

33. theirs

34. This

35. Those

36. This / that

37. These / they

38. This / that

39. This / that

40. What

41. Whom

42. Whom

43. Who

44. Which

SECTION 3 - Reading Comprehension

1. mammal

2. South America

3. place

4. see

5. lazy

6. held

7. spends

8. asleep

9. stays

10. alone

11. A

12. D

13. B

14. B

15. D

SECTION 4 – Writing

Answers vary

Made in the USA
Las Vegas, NV
20 February 2025